The Curious History of VEGETABLES

T0343665

The Curious History of VEGETABLES

Bill Laws

Foreword by Henrietta Green

The
History
Press

Cover illustration: istockphoto.com/Elena Chiplak

First published 2006 as *Spade, Skirret and Parsnip*
This updated paperback edition first published 2024

The History Press
97 St George's Place, Cheltenham,
Gloucestershire, GL50 3QB
www.thehistorypress.co.uk

British Library Cataloguing in Publication Data.
A catalogue record for this book is available from the British Library.

ISBN 978 1 80399 715 5

Typesetting and origination by The History Press
Printed and bound in Great Britain by TJ Books Limited, Padstow, Cornwall

Trees for LYfe

Contents

Gardening Mirrors Life
Foreword by Henrietta Green

Vegetable gardening came comparatively late into my life. If truth be told, no gardening – vegetable or otherwise – figured until, in pursuit of the rural idyll, I moved to Gloucestershire.

London was where I misspent my childhood. Blessed with a large garden, I whiled away hour after hour playing with my Scottie dog Kim or, later on, flirting with my next-door neighbour while he fed his chickens – and yes, he did keep hens and an excessively cock-a-doodling cock in the poshest part of St John's Wood. Gardening was something done by a stream of gardeners.

Even though I never once saw my mother cook a meal, I have enjoyed a happy career as a food writer. Equally, even though I never saw either of my parents wield so much as a pair of secateurs, it has not prevented me from embracing gardening with all the passion of a late convert.

In *The Curious History of Vegetables*, Bill Laws makes me realise what a fascinating pastime I have latterly adopted. With all its irritations, foibles, triumphs and disappointments, gardening mirrors life. Vegetables were the staff of life and, just as snobbery existed in the world at large, so it did in the kitchen garden. Imagine the pressure on the 'gentleman's gardener' who not only had to grow the right vegetables but had to get them to the table at the right time, preferably long before 'poor people even think of such a thing.'

By celebrating our history of vegetables, Bill Laws highlights the facts and foibles for our pleasure and edification. He certainly – if you will forgive the pun – knows his onions. *The Curious History of Vegetables* is a charming read, written with authority, a gentle humour and a superb feel for detail. So next time you get your spade from the shed to dig 'the plot', you may be reassured to know that you are merely one in a long line of vegetable fanatics.

Henrietta Green

The Kitchen Garden

According to Rudyard Kipling the caretaker of the vegetable plot was a patient soul who was to be seen 'grubbing weeds from gravel paths with broken kitchen-knives'. And yet, according to Beatrix Potter and P.G. Wodehouse who each created their own curmudgeonly kitchen gardener apparently based on real-life Victorian or Edwardian gardeners, the vegetable gardener was a tyrant. Yet most of us find the vegetable garden to be that quiet, contemplative sanctuary that Thomas Jefferson enjoyed: 'I have lived temperately, eating little animal food, and that ... as a condiment for the vegetables, which constitute my principal diet,' he explained in 1819.

The kitchen garden is a place to which, like Diocletian, we retire. It is a place of bottom gardens, allotments and potting sheds. It is also a place of quirky and curious revelations. Its tool sheds have been filled with the boys' toys of the garden since at least Queen Victoria's reign, plundered by disgruntled citizens during times of conflict, and raided by at least one poisoner who later met his fate on the gallows. But the potting shed, too, has been a place of retreat – and a base from which to wage war on garden pests especially those celebrated enemies, slugs and snails, which have come in for a range of treatments from the bizarre to the benign.

To make the most of vegetables, they should be eaten as fresh as possible – nothing equals the crispness of home-grown vegetables. However, the trade in fruit and veg is a brisk and lucrative one; the greengrocery or produce aisle is the most profitable one in the supermarket. A business, which was once the slow trade of the costermonger, has developed into a global market where the distance between field and fork has grown to many thousands of air miles. The key to this expanding market is to pick it quick and keep it cool: the business of preserving vegetables has a strange past – and no more so than when it involved Bob Birdseye's discoveries during his days as a fur trapper in Labrador.

The vegetable garden has a long timeline and a curious history, quite as compelling as that of any formal garden. And with world famous kitchen gardens such as Monticello, the home of the American president Thomas Jefferson, in Virginia; Heligan in Cornwall; Winston Churchill's Chartwell in Kent; and Villandry in France, home grown vegetables have become as fashionable as they are fresh.

Contenders for the prize of the world's oldest vegetable include the pea, the lettuce and the bean, while the award for world's most versatile vegetable should, by rights, go to a fruit you can eat, serve food on, and wash with: the squash. When vegetable plots needed to be measured out, standards were set both by the pyramid-building Egyptians and, in the Middle Ages, by the feet of the first sixteen people to leave the village church. Indeed, if it were not for vegetables, the world as we know it today would not exist: both the Spanish and American nations were hot housed on a nutritious, protein-rich diet of maize – cultivated in Mexico around 2,500 years ago, maize is a relative newcomer to the European kitchen garden.

In the beginning was the seed. The traffic in vegetable seeds and the methods of marketing them range from a Shenandoah country and western radio station to modern podcasts and earnest blogs. Coming up with a universal classification for all those seeds and plants fell to Carl Linnaeus and his unfortunate friend Artedi. Linnaeus proved to be as successful as that clever London couple, Mr and Mrs Loudon, who taught the middle classes of the 1800s everything they needed to know about the vegetable.

Vegetable growing comes down to good husbandry, good fences and good, fertile soil. But the kitchen gardener is an anxious soul and inclined to welcome any idea, however eccentric, that might help him or her succeed. The down-to-earth approach works well enough, but over the centuries gardeners have tried some eccentric methods of raising vegetables, from following the moon's quarters to speaking encouraging words to their plants. Painters and clerics, poets and politicians are among those who have sometimes taken their vegetables too seriously. There was the Suffolk clergyman who was convinced that growing vegetables would reduce street crime; and the garden correspondent who claimed that eating potatoes led to verbosity; the American president Woodrow Wilson believed that raising vegetables would cure citizens of their 'extravagant and wasteful' ways while the Victorian critic John Ruskin thought that growing vegetables would better your position in society – and hopefully improve your table manners. The French artist Claude Monet regularly broke from painting another set of water lilies at Giverny to check progress in his kitchen garden next door. And there are those historians who remain convinced that the Roman Empire would have survived if its emperor Diocletian had remained at his post in Rome instead of taking early retirement to grow cabbages at his Illyrian palace. 'Could you but see the vegetables I have raised,' he enthused to a friend even as the empire descended into civil war.

It was these same conquering Italians who gave us the word vegetable from *vegere*, to grow, to animate and to enliven, and the vegetable has continued to inspire ever since. People have grown vegetables in protest against a range of foes from wealthy landowners and multinationals to American military powers. Others, including the Protestants of northern Europe, refused to engage with the potato on religious grounds. The last two world wars led to an understandable passion to Dig for Victory and it was said that home-grown vegetables had rescued Britain ·from the blockade by German submarines in World War Two: *Tuber über Alles*, mocked one Punch cartoonist. And curiously the British people were never so healthy, nor their allotments so full, as they were by the end of the war in 1945.

Emperor Tiberius, John Innes, John Loudon, Rudolph Steiner, Henry Doubleday, Lawrence D. Hills and Popeye: history is full of people with a passion for vegetables. The following forty-eight stories explore that passion – and the curious history of the vegetable from the medieval monastic garden to the full-on frenzy of Covent Garden in its hey day; from the cathedral-like peace of the walled kitchen garden to the bitter battles of the allotment campaigners; from the muck and magic of the organic gardener to the mysteries of compost.

1

Vegetable Husbandry

THE ORIGINS OF THE KITCHEN GARDEN

The kitchen garden, as essential to the well-being of a Palestinian household a thousand years ago as it was to an allotment holder in Pontefract a century ago, has a long, if obscure history. Garden historians tend to celebrate the pleasure grounds and paradise plots of the wealthy rather than those of their lesser yeomen. It does not help that classical writers stayed largely silent on the subject of the vegetable plot. Yet the antiquity of the kitchen garden is incontestable and many still lie, like a host of Heligans, awaiting rediscovery.

In medieval times there was a lexicon of Latin, French and English names for garden places including *gardinium*, *hortus*, *herbarium*, *viridium*, *virgultum* and *vergier*. There was a *wyrtyard*, or little park, and a *herber*, a small ornamental garden with a lawn of less than 1 acre. The medieval kitchen garden was a curtilage, *leac-garth* or *leac-tun* from the Anglo Saxon for *geard*, *tun* or *zeard* meaning a yard or enclosure – this was the 'backyard' that the Elizabethan settlers carried with them to the Americas.

The common root for the word *giardino* in Italian, *jardin* in French, and *garten* in German, is the Old English *geard* or *garth*, an enclosed place or yard. The first mention of a *ketchyngardyn* or *kechengardyn* in Britain appears in the manorial accounts of the Bishop of London in the 1300s. Up until then Europeans kept silent on the subject. The peasant, footstool of the manorial system and mainstay of the medieval economy, had neither the time, skills nor inclination to record anything about his or her methods of growing for the pot. Yet the talents of the peasant gardener ensured that the pottage, a boiled cauldron of vegetables and, occasionally, meat, kept their families alive.

Early European kitchen gardens were little lifelines, fertile plots dedicated to growing the basic necessities. In villages and hamlets across the continent the kitchen garden hugged the house or stood, encircled by earth banks, ditches and stockades, between the cottages and the fields. On the mirey clays of Burgundy or down on the Somerset levels of western England village gardens were raised up above the flood plain and set upon islands surrounded by drainage dykes and the deep, muddy tracks that marked out their boundaries. Ditches, pools and pig wallows were an intrinsic and practical part of the country scene since they manured the ground and watered the vegetables. Unfortunately, they regularly swallowed up the young too. Barbara Hanawalt in *The Ties That Bound* reports that: 'On 29 May 1270 Cicely, aged 2 and a half, went into the yard: a small pig came and tried to take bread from her hand. She fell into a ditch and was drowned.'

Although storable winter staples such as vetches and beans might be sown in strips alongside the orchard where the cutting hay and animal pasture grew, the kitchen garden kept to its conventional 'quarters'. Quartered by a cross of paths, this four-square pattern, edged perhaps with low, clipped hedges of yew, juniper, lavender or dwarf box, was as much part of the kitchen garden scene in ancient Persia as it was to the new Elizabethans of the 1950s growing vegetables in their post-war Surrey suburbs.

Back in Roman times Pliny had already worked out that digging over the 'quarters' of a plot of two-thirds of an acre to a depth of 3ft took eight men a day. But we must wait until 820 before some monk saw fit to commit to parchment the design of a European kitchen garden. This was at the Benedictine abbey of St Gall in Switzerland where the hortus measured a tenth of an acre (404 sq. m) and the different esculents were grown in 5.4m-long rectangular beds each 6m by 1.5m wide.

The Benedictine orders (the Black Monks), the later Cistercians (the White Monks) and Augustinians were as closely wedded to their gardens as they were to their God. Monasteries were centred on the cloistered garth, a patch of grass kept as neat as a bowling green not least because the colour green, as the twelfth-century French prior Hugh of Fouilly put it, 'nourishes the eyes and preserves their vision'. Close by would be the physic garden filled with medicinal plants; a small, locked poison garden where narcotics such as opium poppies, hemlock and mandrake were grown; and the orchard cemetery, a pleasant place for a burial with its air of quiet contemplation and sanctuary.

Finally there was the utilitarian kitchen or cellarer's garden run to the very best of their abilities by a grumbling friar or nun. The Italian Christian St Benedict advised his followers to keep an open house for travellers and to tend the sick and needy. Their peasants paid their tax, a tithe or tenth of his produce, to the clergy. The tax, which was based not only on the field crops and animals, but also the produce of the 'foot-dug' garden, supported the local monastery which served as motel, college, roadside diner, citizen advice bureau and hospital, complete with accident and emergency department. Never sure how many guests might be taking bed and board (the board was literally the supper table) and supping at the monastery that evening, the cellarer needed to keep abreast of the latest developments in the cultivation and storage of their esculents.

A cellarer's garden recreated in the monastic gardens of Shrewsbury and designed by the late Sylvia Landsberg serves to show what the monk Brother Cadfael might have grown. Cadfael, the fictional creation of English author Edith Pargeter (writing as Ellis Peters), was an enthusiastic gardener and herbalist who, like his real ancestors, had gained useful knowledge of the apothecary's art from his travels in the Holy Land. Traditional plots of 1.2m-wide beds were surrounded by 0.6m paths where coleworts, onions, leeks, leaf beet and broad beans were taken to be eaten green. Nitrogen-restoring legumes were an especially useful crop.

Salad, leek and colewort seedlings grew in the nursery bed while the useful fennel, mint, wormwood and hyssop were sown nearby. These last were all good 'strewing' plants for spreading on the floors like some medieval air freshener. Cadfael would also have ensured there was a plentiful supply of flax for linen and bandages, and hemp for rope and sacking.

The kitchen garden was well stocked. In the 1500s the farmer poet Thomas Tusser, author of *Five Hundred Pointes of Good Husbandrie,* lists no less than 1200 plants for the housewife to grow and, while his records included medicinal plants, plants for strewing and scenting hand water and insecticidal plants to keep away the flies, there were plenty of vegetables for the pot. There were brassicas, usually colewort (a kind of cale) and cabbages for the wealthy; parsley, leeks, leaf beet, parsnips, turnips and skirrets; beans and peas, grown to be dried and eaten during the winter; garlic, chives, the 'common bulb onion' and a 'green-leaved one'. In the salad bed the leaves, seeds or petals of a range of self seeding annuals such as borage, marigold, rocket, feverfew and poppy made as pretty a posy as they did when used to fill the salad bowl.

Around the beginning of the 1500s the English kitchen garden was revitalised by the arrival of around 50,000 French protestant Huguenots, fleeing religious persecution in northern Europe. Many of the Huguenots had lived in the Low Countries, in places like Flanders where the local gardeners customarily shipped fresh vegetables across the Channel to Britain. (Peas imported from Holland were reportedly 'fit dainties for ladies, they come so far, and cost so dear', complained one Mr Fuller.) When the Huguenots *réfugiés* themselves sailed for England they brought with them their superior glass and ropework technologies, and their expertise in fruit and vegetable growing. (One of their number, baby Augustine Courtauld, founder of what became the world's largest textile company, arrived hidden in a basket of vegetables.) Herbs and salads, parsley and leaf beet, cucumbers and melons, mint and asparagus (cooked first then eaten cold) were soon growing happily alongside onions, nursery beds of tender young plants and groups of medicinal herbs.

By now Thomas Hill, writing under the curious pseudonym Didymus Mountain, was working on *The Gardener's Labyrinth*, which was published posthumously in 1571. Hill had promised to reveal 'worthy Secretes, about the particular sowing and remouing of the moste Kitchen Hearbes; with the wittie ordering of other daintie Hearbes, delectable Floures, pleasant Fruites, and fine Rootes, as the like hath not heretofore bin vttered of any.' Hill advocated trenched beds, with 1ft-wide trenches on either side to water the beds. (This was not to be confused with the practice of 'trenching' or manuring vegetable beds by digging a deep trench and filling the bottom with manure.)

Well-drained paths were laid to separate the vegetable beds from flower borders filled with useful plants such as marigold, ox eye daisies, carnations and pinks. Intercropping was a useful practice, thought Thomas Hill, with broad beans, early dwarf and the later tall peas grown together, and strawberry runners, planted between rows of onions, being allowed to grow on for harvesting the following year, the onions having been lifted and stored in the autumn.

The kitchen garden, like the formal flower garden, was kept neat. Seed was sown in drills rather than broadcast or sown in patches. For the fastidious kitchen gardener there was the quincunx layout, a method of 'planting in rows, by which the plants in the one row are always opposed to the blanks in the other, so that when a plot of ground is planted in this way, the plants appear in rows in four directions'.

For the time being the gardeners' choice of vegetables was limited to what had been passed down from the Persians, Greeks, Romans, Christian and Christian academics – universities like Toledo, Cordoba, Bologna and Paris had all furthered the development of vegetables as had the great botanical gardens of Pisa, Padua, Parma and Florence. But the growing two-way trade with America was about to bring about an unparalleled transformation to the vegetable patch.

In America intercropping and companion planting was a well-established craft in the communal gardens of the native American people. Corn or maize was sown, after due ceremony and respectful rituals, and fertilised with whatever was available locally whether it was fish and wood ash or bat dung from neighbouring caves. Corn was followed by lima and kidney or pinto beans, the beans using the stems of the maize for support. Then it was the turn of the pumpkins, squashes and sunflowers (for oil) and Jerusalem artichokes (for their storable tubers). The ripening of the first cobs of corn was a cause for celebration and the cobs would be baked in the embers of the fire at the Green Corn Festival. Mature cobs from the later crops would be hung in ropes likes strings of onions and stored in the smoky rafters of the lodge.

The early European settlers were suspicious at first of South America's maize, potatoes, tomatoes, peppers and yams and north America's vegetable marrows, squash, pumpkins, Jerusalem artichokes and beans. But once they and their families had been saved from starvation by the native American crops, they extolled their vegetable virtues and sent the seed home to Europe. It was put to good use. Indian maize was so nutritious that it was said to be responsible for doubling the population of Spain in the 1700s. The potato did the same for the half-starved Irish people whose population rose from 3 million in 1750 to 8 million in 1845 before potato blight triggered the disastrous crop failures.

During the Industrial Age the kitchen garden underwent more radical reforms. Working men grew essential supplies on their allotments; the 'villa' gardener devoted the bottom of the garden to vegetables while those higher up the social scale poured thousands of pounds into prestigious and productive fruit and vegetable gardens. Snobbery was rife – even in the kitchen garden. 'Let us begin with the earliest crops (of peas) which the cottagers seldom aims at; but which the gentleman's gardener and the amateur must produce, so as to have them on the table long before poor people think of such a thing,' recommended the Victorian gardener Shirley Hibberd (1825–1890). The cottager, amateur and gentleman's gardener, who was generally a cottager in his spare time anyway and perfectly capable of raising early peas if he chose, might have every conceivable vegetable at his disposal, but he still had to contend with the seasons. The methods taken to manage the climate marked the next significant change in raising vegetables.

While market growers in the vales of Kent and Evesham concentrated on mass production, research and development fell to those earnest amateurs on their country estates, aided by armies of gardeners. It was no use relying on 'Johnny Foreigner': the prolific garden writer John Claudius Loudon (1783–1843), who viewed European gardeners with despair, explained: 'Horticulture has made little progress in Italy. Forcing or prolonging crops is unknown; everything is sown at a certain season, and grows up, ripens, and perishes together. The red and white beet, salsify, scorzonera, chervil, sorrel, onion, shallot, Jerusalem artichoke, are in many parts unknown', he declared.

It was left to the estate head gardeners to forward vegetable development, exchanging ideas and sharing their knowledge in popular publications such as Loudon's own *Gardener's Magazine*, *Gardeners' Chronicle* and the *Journal of Horticulture and Cottage Gardening*.

Technological developments in iron and glass making, and the advancing science of the heating engineer, gave the Victorians the means to grown any and every vegetable – and send them to the table at almost any time of year. All that was required was money and people power. However, the rumble of canon fire on the battle fields of Flanders was about to bring it all to an end. The Duke of Devonshire's 400-year-old estate at Chatsworth in Derbyshire was a case in point. The great house had been provisioned by a seven-acre kitchen garden aided, by 1905, by almost 2 acres of glass housing. In 1890 the gardeners were assembled for a group photograph in front of the Great Conservatory. There were forty-six of them. Their numbers had been halved by 1917 and shortly after the end of World War One the greenhouses were sold off and plans were drawn up to discontinue the kitchen garden altogether. Death duties, labour costs and, finally, the World War Two would see the greengrocer rather than the gardener provisioning these palaces of the Edwardian and Victorian age.

For the rest of the population, however, urbanisation and the industrial age had reduced city gardens to a fraction of their former selves and there was a saccharine nostalgia for old cottage gardens where radishes and runner beans grew among the roses. Yet amateur gardeners were still cropping vegetables where they could, on allotments or pinched plots of wasteland. People wanted proper gardens.

On the eve of the 1900s a parliamentary reporter and urban planner, Ebenezer Howard (1850–1928), had already given voice to their aspirations. Living in the country, he pointed out, brought 'Beauty of Nature, Bright Sunshine and Abundance of Water', but it was blighted by 'Lack of Society,

Trespassers Beware and Deserted Spirit.' In town the benefits of 'Opportunity, High Money Wages and Places of amusement' had to be offset against 'Closing Out of Nature, Foul Air, High Rents, and Slums and Palaces'. The perfect compromise, argued Howard, was a 'garden city', a place that combined town and country and which boasted 'Beauty of Nature, Social Opportunity, and Fields and Parks of Easy Access, and Homes and gardens'. Howard's reforming garden city ideas paved the way for an era of social housing with gardens and vegetable plots for all. Benevolent industrialists including William Lever at Port Sunlight on Merseyside and George Cadbury at Bournville in Birmingham had already provided vegetable allotments with their workers' homes. Now garden towns modelled on Howard's theories were built at Letchworth from 1903 and Welwyn from 1920. Howard's homes, each with its own garden and vegetable plot, formed a template for housing estates right through the twentieth century, although after the war-time frenzy of vegetable growing, the vegetable plot began to retreat down the gardens. The preserving and packaging industries and the availability of cheap imported vegetables made store-bought produce cheap and attractive.

Then, just as Stuart Dudley was suggesting in the 1960s that it was 'uneconomical in the accepted meaning of the word to keep the kitchen supplied with vegetables from the garden', the kitchen garden started to enjoy a slow revival. There was a whole-food movement and a rise in vegetarianism in the 1960s. In the 1970s students grew vegetables among their cannabis plants on dubious pieces of squatted ground, and hippies, in between protests against the Vietnam war, took over unloved allotments to grow fresh vegetables to accompany their frugal meals of brown rice and bacon bits. There were fastidious bio-dynamic gardeners and organic growers who, frustrated in their search for pesticide-free produce, turned to growing their own. There were city farms and social projects espousing the therapeutic benefits of growing vegetables for people with disabilities. Television, which was overtaking gardening as one of the nation's most popular past times, played its part by creating improbable media celebrities of gardeners like Geoff Hamilton who were more than happy to show a nation how to grow vegetables again. In 1999 the prestigious garden exhibition at Chaumont-sur-Loire was devoted to 'Nothing But Vegetables' and, as rock stars like Paul and Linda McCartney and royals like the then Prince of Wales, later the King of England, reinstated their vegetable gardens, home grown vegetables once again became as fashionable as they were fresh. Championing their cause were celebrity chefs and food activists including Jamie Oliver and Hugh Fernley-Whittingstall who told *The Guardian* newspaper in 2011: 'We need to eat more vegetables and less flesh because vegetables are the foods that do us the most good and our planet the least harm.' Vegetables had become a potential solution to the global crisis of climate change.

TOP FIVE

Favourite Vegetable Seeds

1. Carrot
2. Parsnip
3. Broad Bean
4. Beetroot
5. Cauliflower

Source: Medwyns of Anglesey, specialist seed merchant.

BOUNDARIES, WALLS AND FENCES

Good fences make good neighbours. They also make good kitchen gardens. The need to fence the vegetable plot has exercised gardeners for centuries. Hedges, sunken fences, walls and wide watercourses all played their part.

Water was an effective way to keep predators off the kitchen garden. (It could keep them in too; in medieval times a water-filled ditch was often used to contain the rabbit warren and ensure a supply of fresh meat.) A ready water supply also allowed for regular watering and a place to grow useful willows, rushes and watermint. In pre-Roman Britain, at least, there was no need to fret about rabbit fencing since the coney had yet to be brought to Britain. Long after they had left there were other beasts to worry about. A surplus of wolves (and rioting Welshmen), for example, drove the monks of Llanthony from their monastery in the remote Black Mountains of Wales to the safety of Gloucester in 1135. Once the wolves were gone, marauding deer and cattle might still devour the peasant's winter supplies of leeks and coleworts. While the peasant was pestered by rapacious animals, abbots and abbesses fretted about light-fingered passers-by. Stonewalls were usefully employed to guard the vegetable plot. The oldest dated wall in Britain, at Skara Brae on Orkney, was built around 3,500 years ago, while the silvered stone boundaries that crisscrossed the limestone uplands of Britain were infants by comparison, many dating back to the monastic wool trade of the 1200s and 1300s. The golden limestone walls of the Cotswolds gardens were later additions still. Most date back to the Enclosure Acts of the 1700s and 1800s. The waller's craft varied from region to region, the Cotswold's dry-stone men topping their walls with *combers* while in the Peak District they had a preference for upright coping stones laid in a crenellated, 'cock and hens' style. The Cornishman, meanwhile, favoured an earthen bank reinforced with a herringbone pattern of stone.

Emperor Caesar, pushing through northern Europe during the Gallic wars was impressed by a different type of boundary, the hedge. 'These hedges present a barrier like a wall,' he declared. The living hedge, protected by a ditch to keep browsing cattle at bay, was made by planting saplings of thorn, oak, crab, hawthorn and holly against a temporary stake and pole fence. Within a decade the saplings were tall enough to be laid, when the sap was down, during the winter. The hedger would cut into the lower part of the sapling and bending it over, weave it around fresh stakes cut from surplus hedge timber. The top of the hedge was finished with a whippy rail of willow or hazel and a small willow bed was often planted close by to provide spare parts. As Thomas Tusser pointed out in his *Five Hundred Pointes of Good Husbandrie*: '... euerie (every) hedge/hath plenty of fewell and fruit.'

Anyone caught stealing that 'fewell' faced being whipped until they 'bled well' for the offence of hedgebreaking and to compensate the landowner who would have to call on the hedgemender to make good the damage. (It was said that the figure of a dim-witted hedger shouldering his fork-load of thorns can still be seen on the face of a full moon.) A dead hedge was an acceptable alternative to the living hedge. In Estonia, tall hazel rods, or ethers as they were called in sixteenth-century England, were woven between three horizontal poles; in Sweden pine poles, held together with a twist of bark, rested at 45 degrees in a timber framework; in north and west Wales fangs of slate, waste from the quarries, were stood on end and wired together in a vernacular version of the picket or paling fence (a pale from the Latin *palus* a stake). This boundary fence, so cherished in suburban America, has interesting antecedents. The primary purpose of the 'pale' in the Middle Ages was not to protect the kitchen garden, but to keep fallow deer in their proper place – the nobleman's park. The medieval pale was made of split or cleft oak stakes set in the ground and nailed to horizontal rails and, to make doubly sure the deer stayed in, a bank and ditch were added, the pale fence being run along the top of the bank. (In Ireland, after the conquest of King Henry II, the English settled within The Pale, an area fenced off against the Irish. Those living 'beyond the pale' were beyond redemption). Once the gardener had enclosed his growing plot with hedge, fence or wall, he soon realised an unexpected benefit: a walled garden is a warm garden.

By the time of Queen Victoria's coronation in 1837, the walled kitchen garden was a fashionable favourite, not least because the brick wall raised the temperature within the garden by a good degree or two. A century later, without the workforce required to tend them, these kitchen gardens were crumbling into disrepair. Another half a century on and campaigners were calling for their restoration. Within the walled garden, the conventional square- or rectangular-shaped garden was traditionally quartered by four vegetable plots surrounded by paths and wall-side borders. Their dimensions reflected the size of the household: at Holkham in Norfolk, for example, the walls enclosed no less than 6 acres. Walled gardens were orientated slightly to the west of south so that the heat of the early afternoon was concentrated on one wall. This suntrap, which stored the heat and released it through the chill night, was usually built higher than the other walls so as to make the most of its position. It was a fine site for fruit: figs, vines, peaches, apricots and nectarines would be planted against the south-west walls and late fruiting plums, gooseberries, currants and morello cherries against the north wall.

The garden designer Humphry Repton (1752–1818) liked to design walled gardens with six or seven sides while the gardening author William Robinson (1838–1895) built his walled garden at Gravetye, Sussex in an oval shape. He used dressed stone rather than brick because, he believed, the stone's smooth surface afforded fewer hiding places for voracious insects. In the US Thomas Jefferson (1743–1826) built a serpentine wall around his garden at Monticello in the late 1700s: rounded or crinkle crankle walls, also known as *slangenmuur* or snake walls, were popular briefly in the UK in the late 1700s and early 1800s. The additional wall surface provided extra surface for heating – one garden writer advocated covering the walls in metal to reflect the heat into the garden although there is no evidence that his suggestion was ever put into practice. But in 1755 one Thomas Hitt attacked the whole notion of serpentine walls as 'attended with evils of one kind or other. Though walls built with curves have, in calm seasons the benefit of more heat than others; yet, in windy weather, the winds ... rebounding from side to side, break and destroy the tender branches and blossoms of trees.'

Fires might be lit inside the walled garden to counter frosts; they were even lit beneath the soil to force fruit, but a more effective way to raise the temperature to limit frost damage was to heat the walls themselves. Hot or flued walls were used in kitchen gardens from the mid 1700s, the tell-tale signs for garden historians being the small cast-iron doors or framed stones set in the wall to clean out the flues. Flues in some walls, however, were simply made large enough for chimney sweep's child to climb in and clean while at Fonthill in Wiltshire, the work was carried out, allegedly, by the estate's Jamaican dwarves. Heated walls were eventually superseded by heated glasshouses built against the walls.

Being fire-resistant, cheap and attractive, brick was judged the ideal walling material although other materials included cob, pisé (rammed earth), chalk, timber and even plate glass mounted on iron frames have been tried. Temporary timber walls were another alternative, one design involving deal planks against which a warming pile of manure from the midden was heaped. They were so successful, according to one commentator, that the kitchen gardener could raise 'gooseberries fit for tarts' five months early in January. But dark red, well-fired (and therefore harder and longer lasting) brick was judged best. In Britain the introduction of a tax on bricks in 1750 slowed the pace of walled garden construction, but by 1850, when the tax was repealed, the demands of the country-house guests on the produce of the vegetable garden made the walled kitchen garden as necessary as a polite parlour maid and a deferential butler.

Although the twentieth century saw the walled garden spiral into a near terminal decline, organisations such the Walled Kitchen Gardens Network were formed to save and preserve the remainder. It was a feature worthy of conservation if the recollections of one Herefordshire head gardener, Keith Ruck, were anything to go by:

> There's something about working in a walled garden. The atmosphere is like working in a church: I always remember when the gardens were open to the public and you'd be down there and there'd be hundreds of people milling round. Then, at dusk when they'd gone home and you'd go down to shut some lights up or something, you'd turn in the doorway when you was coming out from there and it almost feels like you got to shut the door quietly. I've heard other old gardeners say the same: you almost think like you got to show a bit of reverence.

A Good Idea at the Time: Blanching

Who knows when the first person noted the effects of blanching their crops? The term started to appear in the late 1700s and before long gardeners were assiduously binding their lettuce leaves together, burying their endive in trenches, and heaping soil or sand around the beet leaves to prevent photosynthesis and produce a sweet, white and tender leaf. Chicory and celery might be buried fresh in barrels of sand (upside down to keep the sand out) until they blanched. Or else they might be enveloped in earth and covered with a warming layer of horse dung. Seakale, which could be blanched in the garden under a clay pot as with rhubarb, was also naturally blanched where it grew on the seashore, by piling beach stones and pebbles around the stems.

Muck and Magic

How do you grow good vegetables? The answer, as one BBC radio comedian Kenneth Williams used to say, lies in the soil. That soil had to be constantly improved and manure was the essential improver. 'Be avaricious for manure, and always keep your mind in firm conviction that your ground is in an impoverished state,' advised Shirley Hibberd. A comprehensive list of manures that have been used from the early 1800s include sea weed, spoiled hay, tanner's spent bark, Cornish pilchards and Fenland sticklebacks, whale blubber ('good reports from Surrey', according to one source), horn and bone, hair, woollen rags, blood, coral, urine, pigeon dung and the dung of domestic fowls, cattle, oxen, sheep, deer and camels, street and road dung, soot, soapers' waste and house sweepings. A Mr Young reported an experiment where a field was spread with herrings and ploughed in for wheat. The crop, however, was 'so rank' it was 'laid before harvest.'

The use of street sweepings continued into the 1920s and 1930s as gardener Keith Ruck recalled:

> In those days around Abergavenny they had the linesman, as they was called, and they used to cut the sides of the road: put the line down and no twists and all done perfect there. The leaves were all swept up and then all that was put in tumps along the side of the road. Some of the farmers had horse and carts under contract to the council for collecting it up. We used to get them to tip it near the bottom of the garden. Then, when that was rotted, we used to sieve it all out and use it for a seed compost.

For a liquid feed Mr. Ruck senior would take an old tar barrel, burn out the remaining tar and fill it with water. 'We used to scrounge round all the farms for when the farmers were dagging, that was cleaning the rear ends of lambs and sheep before shearing. We used to collect all those, put 'em in a hessian sack and hang them in the barrel. That was our liquid feed. You couldn't beat it.'

For solid manuring, the vegetable garden was double dug or trenched, a method involving digging a trench two 'spits' of a

spade deep (a spit being the length of the spade blade), laying
the bottom of the trench with well-rotted manure and covering the trench with soil excavated from the next row along. A
bed might be trenched every four or five years. Some writers,
possibly those who could pay the gardener to do it for them,
advocated a back-breaking trench three spits deep.

Another way to keep the ground in good heart was to leave a
plot fallow for a year. The term fallow, as in fallow deer, referred
to the pale red or pale-yellow colour of land, which had been
turned or ploughed, but left unsown.

Apart from perennials such as Jerusalem artichokes or asparagus, most vegetables in the northern hemisphere were planted
in spring. Half the crop – onions, peas, beans and salads – was
harvested within six months, and the remainder over the rest of
the year. A rule of thumb to avoid the ground 'getting tired' was
never to follow a crop with another of the same family. 'A stud-
ied rotation is advisable. The kitchen garden should be divided
into a number of portions, and a journal or notebook should
be kept, with a reference to their numbers,' advised one head
gardener, Mr Walter Nicol, in his *The Forcing, Fruit and Kitchen
Gardener* of 1802.

Through the 1900s the more intensive, four crop rotation saw
potatoes, legumes, brassicas and roots trooping after one another
around the plots. Heavy manuring and deep digging for the
potato crop benefited the beans and peas that followed. Their
nitrogen fixing roots aided the growth of the brassicas that followed while the final root crop would grow straight and true. In
his classic *Organic Gardening* (1977) Lawrence D. Hills advocated
a four-crop rotation with four beds to fit into a standard allotment or 'two beds, one on each side of the centre path of the
average 1930s-built semi-detached house garden.' His practical
description evokes the suburban back garden with its 'cropping
space, bush fruit, herb bed near the kitchen door, tool shed and
compost bin behind the garage, and the lawn crossed by the
clothes line.'

Back in medieval times, while every good gardener knew how to fertilise the soil, horticulturists were hard pressed to explain the process. The German theologian Cardinal Nicolas of Cusa (1401–1464), who weighed soil and plant before and after the crop matured, discovered that the soil's weight had altered little. Water, he concluded, played a significant part in the process.

In the 1200s scientists at the University of Bologna experimented with seeds and plants in the hope that their discovery might lead to their being able to turn base metals into gold. The secret of soil fertility was still something of a holy grail for the alchemists of the 1500s and 1600s. The Germans were first past the finishing post when, in the mid 1800s, Justus von Liebig (1803–1873) revealed that plants took in carbonic acid, water, ammonia, potassium, calcium, magnesium, phosphate and sulphate, converting them into starch, sugar, fat and proteins. Furthermore, he confirmed that animals, which ate and excreted plants, returned these elements to the soil. He was nearly, but not quite there, and it fell to the German botanist Julius Sachs (1832–1897) to identify the essential minerals. His list omitted actual soil and in 1860 he astonished the horticultural world by growing plants soil-less, hydroponically in mineral-fed water.

Then, after two German chemists studying sugar beet discovered how plants take up nitrogen, John Bennet Lawes (1814–1900) and Joseph Gilbert (1817–1901) working at Lawes' family home, Rothamsted Manor in Hertfordshire, devised the ingredients for an artificial fertiliser. Within half a century gardeners were producing remarkable results with their new chemicals: nitrate of soda, nitrate of potash or sulphate of ammonia, sulphate of potash, superphosphate of lime. Potash developed the sugars and starches in potatoes and tomatoes especially while nitrogen inputs were fast working and produced vigorous green plants. But there was a spectre on the horizon. When scientists revealed that the once useful pesticide Dichloro-diphenyl-trichloroethane or DDT had entered the global food chain, vegetable gardeners began to wonder what they were doing to their soils – and to themselves. The garden world was becoming a potentially poisonous place with residuals such as antibiotics, copper, pesticides, herbicides, cadmium and lead lurking in modern manures and composts. The indications were that the high productivity produced by chemical fertilisers and fearsome pesticides in the kitchen garden could prove to be environmentally damaging. Many turned to the organic lobby and the prophet of the new organic age Lawrence Hills. 'The most important reason for growing as much as possible of our own fruit and vegetables,' he wrote in 1971, 'is to contract out of the race between resistant strains of pests and ever more deadly pesticides and to stop the build-up of these cumulative poisons in the sea, the soil, and the bodies of all living creatures including Man.'

In the 1970s with high inflation and the rising food costs Hills predicted that many would be forced to try for self-sufficiency 'as peasants do in many countries'. He showed that with skilled gardening and a rotation that cropped food through the winter, the 300 square yards of the standard allotment could 'produce nearly a ton and a half of food in a year'. There were plenty of people ready to try. And their first task was to master the mysteries of the compost heap.

THE COMPOST HEAP

Kitchen gardeners agonise over compost heaps in the way that sailors obsess over knots and truck drivers argue over sat-nav recommended routes. The process of composting is child's play: construct a mound of green matter and, given time, anaerobic activity will transform it into an enriching soil improver. Yet social media is awash with plaintive cries: 'mine's full of red worms! A rat's moved in! It's gone mushy!'

Shirley Hibberd extolled the virtue of composting back in Victorian times: 'You have one source of the very best manure in the household, and you must treasure every scrap of stinking rubbish, solid and liquid, and not waste so much as a dead cabbage leaf,' he trumpeted. And so they did: gardeners collected highway manure, grass, weeds, ditch mud, leaves, soot-ashes, household refuse and mixed them together as Hibberd advised 'in the dunghill, and turned frequently before using'.

A century later reluctant domestics were still being sent out into the street with a shovel and bucket when the horse-drawn dray passed by, but by 1941 war-time gardener writer Arthur J Simons was reminding readers: 'The increasing shortage of stable manure, arising out of the decay of horse transport and the difficulty of obtaining any kind of animal manure in and around towns ... have combined to encourage the conversion of vegetable waste of the garden into manure by the making of compost heaps.' Simons was a compost enthusiast and he went on to describe no less than six different methods of making a compost including the 'Quick Return' and the Indore method, a layering technique developed by Shropshire botanist, Sir Albert Howard working with his Indian colleague agriculturalist Yeshwant D. Wad.

The key to the fermentation of a compost heap made of vegetable matter, soil, water and air is the presence of nitrogen which acts as a starter and accelerates the digestion of material into humus. Dung, rich in phosphates, and urine, rich in nitrogen and potash, are powerful activators. But which dung to use? The best, insisted the Muslim gardeners of Spain in the 1400s, came from the best animals: the manure of a corn-fed stallion was infinitely preferable to that of the tired packhorse grazed on poor hay. Others placed bird dung at the top of the list, not least because the dung and urine were so neatly packaged into one dropping: journals from St Peter's in Gloucester record that the mountains of dove droppings from inside the dovecote or columbaria were shovelled out on to the garden twice a year. And there was no point in wasting good urine: in the 1300s Ibn Bassal advised that labourers be encouraged to urinate on the compost. The Roman Columella commended human urine especially if it was be stored for six months and mixed with 'old oil lees' before being applied to the olive crop. Lawrence Hills valued the droppings of horse, cow, pig, chicken and rabbit, declaring 'goat manure is perhaps the best general manure of the lot, because the goat is a browser rather than a grazer ... but the finest activator manure of all is pigeon droppings.'

Vegetable soil could also be 'sweetened' by the products of the privy or privy chamber, that is until the water closet heralded the welcome demise of the city cesspit. (King Henry III ordered 'a privy chamber' to the Queen's garderobe in 1296.) However, in the manure-deprived 1940s Arthur Simons recommended returning to the use of night soil for the compost heap. Night 'soil' (referring to the French *souiller* to sully or defile rather than the upper stratum of the earth) was commonly removed from the earth closet or cesspit under the cover of darkness: 'About once a year a Negro we called Mister Elsey would come with his wagon and clean the vault of our privy,' recalled the American Carl Sandburg quoted in John Pudney's *The Smallest Room*. 'His work was always done at night. He came and went like a shadow in the moon.' In England in the Middle Ages it was the work of the gong fermors (gong meaning a privy and fermors from the verb fey to cleanse) who carried out the task and there was much argument over how long such manure should be allowed to 'ferment' before it was dug into the kitchen garden. By the 1800s 'desiccated night-soil' was being sold in France as *poudrette* while in London, it was mixed with quick-lime, moulded into cakes and marketed as Clarke's Desiccated Compost. Asia small-holders also sold cakes of night soil, mixed with earth, according to one admiring commentator who declared the Chinese 'have more practical knowledge of the use of manures than any other people existing.'

In Britain the industrial revolution saw inventors endeavouring to mechanise the process of making human manure safe for the vegetable plot. In 1860 the vicar of Fordington Rev. Henry

Moule took time out from his parish duties in Dorset to patent the Moule's Earth-Closet device, a clever concept that automatically discharged a quantity of dry earth into the latrine when pressure was exerted on the lavatory seat. Initially sales were sluggish since the contraption required a plentiful supply of dry, finely sifted earth (a special earth drying and sifting stove was soon being marketed for the purpose), but it was widely adopted – and copied – by the British Raj in India.

The Rev. Moule, his wife and eight sons, would like others of his class, expect the morning maid to empty the chamber pots daily on to the garden compost heap since the compost heap was, and still is, the ideal way to return to the soil as much organic matter as possible. (Country clergymen were careful guardians of the compost heap and at least one Midlands rector is known to have enriched his with a little of the crematorium remains that came into his care before the subsequent funeral.) Decomposing vegetation is home to millions of soil organisms that feed the soil, improve drainage on heavy soils and help retain water on light soils. With or without Arab stallion urine, *poudrette*, or funeral ashes, it is still judged to be a horticultural wonder.

JOHN INNES' REVOLUTIONARY POTTING COMPOST

John Innes was to the garden what the Hoover was to the home thanks to the potting compost which bore his name. (This 'compost' refers not to the contents of the compost heap, but the mix of materials used in the sowing and raising of seedlings and bulbs.) Born in 1829, Innes went on to become a wealthy London property developer and land dealer and on his death in 1904 he left £325,000 for the founding of a horticultural research centre. The John Innes Horticultural Institute opened in Surrey, and was moved later to Norwich in Norfolk. Contrary to popular belief, the Institute never produced a gram of commercial potting composts – but it did invent the first successful formula.

It had been common for gardeners to rely on their own recipes for special pot soils in which to grow seeds, slips (a twig cut for planting) and cuttings. A Mr Cushing who worked at a nursery in Hammersmith, London in 1812, divulged his own formula to the readers of *Exotic Garden*:

> Loam, peat, and sand, seem to be the three simples of nature, if I may so call them, most requisite for our purpose; to which we occasionally add as mollifiers, vegetable or leaf mould, and well rotted dung; for the judicious mixture and preparation of which, composts may be made to suit plants introduced from any quarter of the globe.

The gardener's stock was often summarily destroyed by some soil-borne disease since these composts were rarely sterilised. Too much fertiliser added to the compost caused the plants to grow leggy and 'soft' or weak; too little and they grew 'hard' or too slow. The John Innes composts were considered just right. Devised in the 1930s, they were based on a mix of seven parts of soil or loam, three parts of peat and two of grit. They were the work of two researchers at the Institute, William Lawrence and John Newell who had been increasingly frustrated in their efforts to grow standard Chinese primroses (*Primula sinensis*) for research purposes in various composts. In the end they devoted six years to perfecting their standard composts, one for seed sowing and one for potting.

The John Innes Number 1, for sowing seed, rooting soft cuttings and pricking out or potting up young seedlings or rooted cuttings, carried only a small amount of nutrients. Number 2, for the general potting of vegetable plants and houseplants into medium sized pots or boxes, contained double the amount of fertiliser. The nutrients, nitrogen for top growth, phosphates for root growth, potash for flowering and fruiting, and trace elements for colour and flavour, were perfectly balanced.

The basic ingredient, loam was made from rotted-down, stacked turf, which was sterilised before being added to sphagnum moss, extracted from peat bogs, and coarse sand or grit to provide the right amount of drainage. Later John Innes No 3 was introduced with a richer mixture for final re-potting of heavier feeding vegetables such as cucumbers and tomatoes, and mature plants and shrubs in interior planters or outdoor containers.

The composts became an industry standard and revolution-ised the growing of seeds and plants in pots. Fifty years later, although the nutrients had changed, the basic formula remained the same until the Great Peat Scandal broke. Peat bogs, vital wildlife wetlands that harbour locked-in carbon, were being mined out for both the amateur and the professional horticul-tural markets. Initially opposed by environmentalists because of the unsustainable damage being done to the peat bogs, peat extraction nevertheless continued to accelerate. Government inaction resulted in 94% of Britain's lowland peat bogs being destroyed by 2013.

By now peat was not only the significant ingredient in potting composts, but being piled on the soil as a cheap and ineffective soil conditioner. Richard Sudell in his *New Illustrated Gardening Encyclopaedia,* published in the early 1900s, had already warned that the acidic nature of peat caused plants to 'fail for want of nourishment.' As he pointed out 'garden refuse if treated intel-ligently can be used as a valuable fertiliser' echoing the more stentorian command of Hibberd not to 'allow the daily waste of the most fertilizing substance that can be had, equal in every way to stable dung' which 'to preserve would cost you noth-ing:' household vegetable waste. By the 2020s governments wavered over a ban, while the horticultural industry stepped in with peat-free composts for the amateur gardener. The substi-tutes included bark, wood fibre, bracken, sheep's wool and green waste compost. Shirley Hibberd was finally vindicated.

VEGETABLE DIVAS

Plants are not sentient beings. They do not flee from the chain-saw or hide from the chomping snail. As if to emphasise this lack of sentience we describe any poor unfortunate who lost all neurological function as being in a vegetable state. And yet while the ancient Greek philosopher Aristotle concluded that vegetables were incapable of experiencing sensations, they did, he insisted, possess souls. In the 1900s a Viennese biologist, Raol Francé, declared that not only did vegetables and other plants move about freely, although on a time scale too slow for us to follow, they were also highly sensitive to either abuse or gratitude. A century later the Israeli botanist Daniel Chamovitz, author of *What A Plant Knows*, considered how the burr cucumber (*Sicyos angulatus*) could detect and respond to a tiny weight placed upon it. In human terms that would be like feeling a lover's kiss as a slap in the face. Peter Tompkins and Christopher Bird (*The Secret Life of Plants, 1973*) controversially considered the sensibility of sunflowers which turned, like incautious sun bathers, to face the sun as it travelled from east to west (hence their French name *tour de sol* and Italian *girasol*) concluding 'plants may ... be the bridesmaids at a marriage of physics and metaphysics.'

Three idealistic English vegetable growers had already concluded that plants were sufficiently sentient to have allies in the spirit world. They were an ex-Royal Air Force squadron leader, Peter Caddy, his wife Eileen and their friend Dorothy MacLean. The three had been running the Cluny Hotel in Scotland during the 1950s when they embarked upon a major life change. Moving to a scruffy caravan site in a remote part of north Scotland which looked out across Findhorn Bay, they were determined to turn aside from the materialist world and pursue a life of 'limitless love and truth'. Central to their aspirations was the raising and growing of vegetables.

There are diminishing returns to be had from most vegetables the further north you travel. Shorter growing seasons and fewer growing days, earlier and later frosts, and poor or indifferent soils all play a part. Peter Caddy found the soil at Findhorn as 'fine, dusty sand and gravel in which nothing grew but rough pointed grass'. Nevertheless, he double dug the plot, laying the up-turned turves at the bottom of the trench and erected a wind proof fence, recycled from a dismantled garage. The land was manured with seaweed and the produce of the compost heap.

The women, meanwhile, sought spiritual guidance. Eileen, who had renamed herself Elixir, spoke of her midnight meditations and her vision of the run-down caravan park being transformed into a place with seven cedar wood bungalows. Dorothy became Divina. In their first year Divina, Elixir and the more prosaic Peter harvested onions, leeks, garlic, carrot, parsnip, swede, turnip, artichoke, kohlrabi, celery, marrow, potatoes, over twenty different kinds of salad and various herbs. In the autumn they pickled 6.75kg of red cabbage, bottles of cucumbers and put potatoes, carrots, beetroot, shallot, onion and garlic in store for the winter. In 1964 Peter Caddy grew a cabbage that weighted 20.25kg. A single sprouting broccoli fed the groups for weeks and was said to be too heavy to lift.

When Sir George Trevelyan, a leading member of the Soil Association and doyen of the New Age, visited the site, he was amazed at the fertility, growth and taste of the vegetables. Peter Caddy revealed the Findhorn secret: Divina had made spiritual contact with whole hierarchies of plant spirits, or devas, who instructed her on how to make the most of the vegetables. She expounded on the theory that you are what you eat, explaining that plants fed the soul as well as the body: vegetables grown by a bad-tempered gardener, for example, could themselves cause ill humour in those who ate them.

'You are perfectly free to say this is nonsense,' Trevelyan would later say in an interview. 'Here you are in the middle of the twentieth century and we're talking of fairies in your garden. But how else do you explain the plants that grow on these decayed sand dunes?'

Within ten years Elixir's premonitions were fulfilled. Findhorn went on to become an established community of 300 people, wealthy enough to buy up the caravan park and replace the caravans with the seven cedar wood bungalows predicted by Elixir. Even the old Cluny Hill Hotel, as well as neighbouring properties, were purchased to house the expanding educational charity of Findhorn. The Findhorn vegetables had proved to be a strange success.

Rudolph Steiner's Biodynamic Vegetables

In 1982 the retiring Director of Agriculture for Tanganika wrote a book called *Bio-Dynamic Gardening*. John Soper had been a dutiful servant of the British colonial service. He had spent thirty-two years in East Africa and Malaya. Captured by the Japanese during World War Two he was a prisoner of war for three and a half years. In his retirement he was to promote some unorthodox ideas on vegetable husbandry.

'More and more people today,' he wrote, 'are convinced in their heart that the world which we see and hear around us is not the only one; behind it and beyond the range of our senses there must be other worlds which underlie, inform, permeate and organise all our natural surroundings.'

When Soper retired to work his own vegetable and fruit patch, first in Hampshire and later at Clent, near Birmingham, he became a leading member of the Bio-Dynamic Association, a movement founded on the teachings of Rudolph Steiner.

Steiner, the son of an Austrian station master, was born in 1861 and died in 1925. By the age of eight he had already experienced 'the reality of the spiritual world'. In his forties he was devoting himself to the 'science of the spirit', or what he called anthroposophy. His writings and teachings helped found the

Camphill villages, devoted to the care of people with learning disabilities, and Waldorf schools as well as methods of bio-dynamic farming and gardening.

In the 1920s Steiner's supporters were as concerned about agricultural trends as consumers were in the 1980s and when he presented a series of lectures on farming in 1924, his ideas on agriculture were adapted to form the basis of bio-dynamic vegetable gardening. Even ardent followers like Soper, however, found Steiner's notions difficult to follow: 'He emphasised that he was speaking from his personal experience on small peasant farms, and he did not mention gardens at all,' wrote Soper later. Nevertheless, the bio-dynamic movement, based at Goetheanum in Dornach, Switzerland, would go on to influence vegetable growers around the world.

'The earth breathes, it has a respiratory system, it has a pulse, it is sensitive and it has a skin,' explained Soper. If that skin was 'broken', by an accidental landslide or a deliberate cut created for a road or railway line, the earth would, in time, heal itself with a protective layer of vegetation. Furthermore, said Soper, since this earthly life form expanded and contracted like any breathing being the gardener should try to work in harmony with its rhythms. For example, plants that bore their crops above ground would grow better when sown during a waxing moon while root crops would thrive when sown as the moon waned. Harvesting leaf vegetables or transplanting seedlings was best done in the mornings as the earth awoke and expanded, while small plants were better transplanted, seeds were better sown, and root crops were better harvested during the evenings, in harmony with the earth as it gently contracted.

Equally important to the growth of vegetables was the influence of the planetary rhythms. The parts of the plant (root, leaf, flower and fruit) mirrored the elements (earth, water, air and light) and each came under the influence of the moon, sun and the zodiac, that ring of twelve constellations against which the sun appears to move in the course of a year. Esoteric perhaps, but

Soper pointed out how vegetables in the northern hemisphere grew to their climax as the sun drove on towards its summer solstice and then waned and ripened as it headed towards the autumn equinox. The moon, he argued, was a mighty influence.

Others had already been studying the lunar influence: 'Most authorities agreed that seed should be sown with a waxing moon,' insisted one writer in the 1800s. Native Americans sensibly looked for the star cluster Pleiades, or the Seven Sisters, to disappear from the spring sky before planting their seed since this signaled the beginning of frost-free nights. In England in the 1690s the author of the *Systema Agriculturae* John Worlidge warned farmers to be mindful of the moon. He declared, for example, that turnips or onions, sown when the moon was full, would not 'bulb out', but send up flower stalks instead, and that a weak tree should be pruned as the moon waxed and a strong one as it waned: 'The most principal of natural causes of all changes and variations of the seasons of the year, and of the different degrees of Heat, Cold, Driness, Etc in those seasons, are first the Sun, then the *Moon*.'

Not everyone agreed. In 1693 the French author of *The Complete Gardener*, Jean-Baptiste de La Quintinie, dismissed the theory. 'I solemnly declare that after a diligent observation of the moon's changes for thirty years together, and an enquiry whether they had any influence in gardening, the affirmative of which has been so long established among us, I perceived that it was no weightier than old wives' tales, and that it had been advanced by unexperienced gardeners. Sow what sorts of grains you please, and plant as you please, in any quarter of the moon, I'll answer for your success, the first and last day of the moon being equally favourable.'

In the early 1800s Loudon, too dismissed the lunar influence as 'superstitious observances attendant on a rude state of society'. And yet the twentieth-century Cornishman John Harris, head gardener at the 22-acre Tresillian House near Truro, was so convinced of the benefits of 'moon gardening' that he wrote a book about it. 'Moon gardening is not about doing more work, it's about doing the right work,' he explained, adding: 'Moon gardening makes you more thoughtful and observant in general.'

Aside from considering the planets, bio-dynamic gardeners also needed to familiarise themselves with their soil. A simple initial test involved taking a fist-full of moist earth and squeezing it into a lump: a sandy soil would fall apart, a clay soil form into a lumpy ball. A second test involved mixing a soil sample with water in a glass jar, shaking it up and allowing it to settle. Sand would fall to the bottom while clay formed a sludge-like mix at the top.

Having established the nature of their soil, the bio-dynamic gardener could then cultivate it with respect since, on planet earth, every gardener and every garden was an individual. Deep digging and trenching was reserved for heavy clay soils while light, sandy soils required little cultivation and benefited from being sheltered from the elements with a cover crop of weeds when it lay fallow.

Horticultural pesticides and artificial fertilisers were to be avoided: 'One fact does appear to be fairly certain,' wrote Soper. 'The effects are partially or wholly negatived by the use of artificial fertilisers and agricultural poisons which deaden the soil's sensitivity and responsiveness.' Instead, the bio-dynamic gardener should 'enliven' the soil with special composts or manures. The preparations were positively sacramental. Preparation 500, for example, involved meditatively stirring 45 grams of 'horn manure', made from cow dung, for an hour in about three gallons of lukewarm water. The container had to be free from all forms of contamination, the water was best taken from a spring, and the stirring stick had to be chosen to 'suit personal convenience'. Even the stirring method was specific: 'Stir briskly until a deep crater is formed in the rotating liquid; then quickly reverse the direction of stirring and continue until the deep crater is formed once more.' The aim was to create a whirling liquid 'in a seething, chaotic turbulence' and the concoction had to be used within the hour, either sprayed on to the garden or flicked out of a bucket with a bunch of twigs, 'the main purpose [being] to stimulate and enhance the supersensible forces and influences working in from the far spaces of the cosmos and up from the centre of the earth.'

Soper's explanation for the benefits of this enlivening mixture proved a step too far for most vegetable growers and yet the basics of biodynamics – helping to heal the earth, especially in the kitchen garden – proved to have a universal appeal. Now involved in related issues such as animal welfare, genetically modified food and sustainable farming, the international movement founded on Steiner's theories and Soper's interpretations still shows no sign of running out of new recruits.

FABULOUS KITCHEN GARDENS

A century ago the idea of opening the kitchen garden to interested visitors would have seemed as odd as offering public tours of the coal cellar. The flower garden and shrubbery were the proper place for decorative delights, not the functional workplace that was kitchen garden. Yet now gardens open to the public are inclined to include a kitchen garden in the tour; some like Heligan and Audley End have founded their reputations on their vegetable borders. Clearly people are genuinely interested in the plantings, the patterns and the structures of the vegetable plot.

While there is no economic imperative for people in America and northern Europe to grow their own fruit and vegetables (as there is during any downturn in the economy), waiting lists for allotments continue to grow in proportion to the scale of protests (even from non-gardeners) whenever plans are unveiled to redevelop them. Garden fashion has played its part in stimulating this vegetal interest, from the Arts and Crafts garden, where a trellis work of runner beans forms part of the romance,

to William Robinson's and Gertrude Jekyll's popularising of
the cottage garden with its intimate mix of flowers, fruit and
vegetables.

Then there are the increasing number of cross over vegetables such as ruby chard, orach or even a plain pattern of lettuce,
which add a frisson of interest to the increasingly informal
flower border. But perhaps there is a more basic reason for this
preoccupation with the fruits of the vegetable plot: people like
to grow what they eat, and eat what they grow.

A glimpse into how a medieval kitchen garden might have
looked is to be found at **Bayleaf**, an old, rescued farmhouse set
in the grounds of the Weald and Downland Open Air Museum
in West Sussex. The garden, researched by the late garden historian Dr Sylvia Landsberg and recreated in front of the house,
was designed with six plots of vegetables worked in a three-year
rotation. Leeks, leaf beet and parsley are planted in the first year,
coleworts or collards in the second, while in the third year the
plots are manured during the winter then planted with onions
the following spring. In summer all the plots come alive with
colour as the undercrop of edible weeds, which are allowed to
self seed each year, come into flower.

In the 1850s Queen Victoria made a handsome £50,000
from the sale of the old kitchen gardens at Kensington Palace,
London. The money did not linger long in the royal coffers.
The Queen and her husband Albert ploughed it back into a new
kitchen garden at **Windsor**. Founded on the same principles as
any other manor house kitchen garden of the time, it was built
with a walled garden, hot houses and tools sheds. The scale of
the enterprise, however, set it apart from the common lot.

One hundred and fifty gardeners worked within the 3.6m-
high outer and inner walls that encircled the 27-acre garden – it
was eventually expanded to 50 acres. In place of conventional
gates, a porter's gatehouse lead into the gardens. The head gardener lived on site in a house with a special suite of rooms where
Albert and Victoria could enjoy a cream tea with fresh – very

fresh – strawberries when they visited. There was an under gardener's house too, built close to over 240m of hot houses. There were boiler rooms, potting sheds, mushrooms houses, forcing pots, stables and, as a centrepiece for the garden, a fountain set in a 9m-diameter basin.

The post-war fate that befell so many kitchen gardens would dispatch Victoria and Albert's kitchen garden too, leaving only its great walls behind. However, a century later in 1980 another member of the British royal family was planning a kitchen garden at his country house, **Highgrove** in Gloucestershire.

King Charles, then the Prince of Wales, took advice from one of his neighbours, the garden author and lecturer Rosemary Verey. Her Cotswold manor home garden at Barnsley House was a model of the twentieth century English Arts and Crafts style with its mixed borders, formal *potager*, classical temple and modern knot. She had also established a decorative vegetable garden based on the designs of William Lawson's *Country Housewife's Garden* of the 1600s (and prompted a revival in the popularity of ruby chard). A new kitchen garden was constructed at Highgrove similarly laid out as a decorative *potager*. Appropriately enough, given the spirit of the new age, the vegetable garden was to be run on organic lines.

'Received from Mr Bryan £3.9s.4d for month's wages, also notice to leave at end of next month', wrote William Cresswell in 1874. He was under gardener at **Audley End** near Saffron Walden in Essex. His diary, which petered out when he left Audley End, gave an insight into the life of the Victorian under gardener. William Cresswell had already contemplated leaving: 'Mr Bryan angry for not sending for him. Self troubled in mind with several things lately taken place in affair connected with situation, had thought of giving notice to leave.'

Twenty-two years old when he arrived from Cambridge to work at Audley End, William Cresswell lived in the bothy next to the great glasshouses (one of the oldest and largest in the UK), enjoying the benefits of central heating from the hot water pipes that ran through the bothy and into the greenhouses. Attached to the stately Jacobean manor house of Audley End the walled vegetable garden, with over two miles of box hedging around the plots, fell into disuse in the World War Two when house and grounds were passed into the hands of the state. Now restored by the Henry Doubleday Research Association, the UK's organic gardening association, and English Heritage, the gardens are open to the public and productive once again.

There are two Hampton Courts in England. The first, and more famous, is the Royal Palace near London, its gardens opened to the public by Queen Victoria in 1838. The second, in the rural West Midlands, features an imaginative decorative kitchen garden. It opened its gardens to the public in the 1990s.

Hampton Court was founded in the early 1400s after the owner, Sir Roland Leinthall, 'toke many prisoners' at the battle of Agincourt, 'by which prey he beganne the new buildings of Hampton Court', according to one commentator. The manor followed the fortunes of many a rich manor house, one moment in favour and the subject of vast expenditure, at another in the doldrums, languishing in decay. The estate was purchased and sold by a succession of owners including knights, a viscountess, a Member of Parliament and a petro-chemical multinational, before being rescued by a wealthy American couple.

In 1810 the estate, which had changed hands only once in the previous four centuries, was bought by Richard Arkwright, said to be 'the wealthiest commoner in England' after his father made his fortune in the cotton industry. However, the upkeep of the estate would drain the resources of three generations of the family over the next century. In the 1840s Joseph Paxton, architect of the Crystal Palace for the Great Exhibition in London, designed a new conservatory. At the close of the century owner Johnny Arkwright patented a successful design for a wooden box made to carry vegetables and fruit without damaging the contents. It was not enough to restore the wealth of the Arkwrights who sold up in 1911. The house changed hands six more times before Americans Robert and Judith Van Kampens bid unsuccessfully for the estate at auction. Nevertheless, they visited the house out of curiosity in 1994, met the vendors and within ten minutes had agreed a sale.

The Van Kampens spent $17.5 million on the restoration of the house and gardens. The Van Kampen gardens, designed by artist and gardener Simon Dorrell were hailed as one of the most ambitious garden creations of the 1990s. The design included a maze of a thousand yews with a gothic tower at its centre. Below the tower an underground tunnel led to a waterfall and a sunken garden. But key to the design were the flowers and decorative vegetables laid out within the original Victorian garden walls and divided up by canals, a pair of octagonal pavilions and pleached tree avenues. Organic produce from the kitchen garden was used to supply a restaurant housed in Paxton's now restored greenhouse. When Robert Van Kampen died in 1999, Hampton Court was eventually sold to business tycoon Graham Ferguson Lacey who promised to keep the Castle open so that the public could continue to enjoy this extraordinary vegetable garden.

In 1772 the kitchen garden at **Clumber Park** near Worksop in Nottinghamshire supplied fresh vegetables and fruit to the 100 strong household of the Dukes of Newcastle. Garden walls enclosed around 4 acres of land, but there was another 6 acres of ground under fruit and vegetable cultivation. It included an acre of glass housing, forcing sheds and mushroom houses. Close by a pair of ice houses were used to store fresh produce. Even in the early 1900s the gardens required twenty-nine full-time gardeners to grow and harvest crops from everyday carrots and potatoes to exotics such as chillies, sweet corn, pineapple and sugar cane.

The manor house was destroyed in a series of disastrous fires, but remarkably the vegetable gardens and chapel were saved. Now the National Trust and a team of volunteers manage the old kitchen garden, its 137m-long glass house, and the National Collection of rhubarb along with raising organic vegetable crops as they would have been grown in the late eighteenth century.

What was to become one of the most famous vegetable gardens of the twentieth century started life as a kitchen garden in the late 1700s. Henry Hawkins Tremayne had been curate of Loswithiel in Cornwall when he unexpectedly inherited an estate. It was called The Willows, but went by the Cornish name for willow, **Heligan**. The family estate, which stretched from Gorran to Mevagissey, was spread across 100 acres of south-west Cornwall. It was large enough to encompass several farms, its own flour mill, brick works, sawmill, brewery and a kitchen garden of nearly 2 acres. Produce from the garden not only helped to feed the family and their guests, but also the twenty inside staff and up to twenty-two outside staff. Henry Tremayne busied himself with Heligan, laying out the gardens more or less as they appear today. Three further generations carried on the horticultural work forward until June 1914 when two shots from an assassin's pistol in faraway Sarajevo sounded what was to be the opening salvo of World War One. It's doubtful whether Heligan's water boy or flowerpot cleaner knew anything about the incident, but already the political repercussions were rippling across Europe. By August of that year, they were lapping up against the walls of the big house.

'Don't come here to sleep or slumber', scribbled one of the gardeners on the lavatory wall as each of his mates signed their name and added the date: August 1914. By the time of the hollow victory of Armistice Day in 1918, three out of every ten British males who had been aged between twenty-four and thirteen at the outbreak of war were dead: they included half the staff of Heligan. Heligan, like so many other grand houses, went into a post war decline.

That was until one winter's day in 1999 when entrepreneurs Tim Smit and John Nelson went exploring and stumbled upon what Smit would later describe as the horticultural equivalent of the Marie Celeste. 'John and I stumbled across a tiny room buried under fallen masonry in a heavy shrouded corner of the walled garden. Here we found those barely legible signatures in its faded, lime-washed walls'.

Ambitiously they decided to restore Heligan. Early efforts were concentrated on the glasshouse fruits and the famous pineapple pit, but it was the 1.8-acre vegetable garden which became what Tim Smit called the engine room of the house. Whole trees and brambles 4m high were cleared from the plot. After ploughing and laying the water pipes, the classic cruciform of paths was relaid and, under the shade of fruit hoops, the four quarters of the vegetable garden were restored.

The Heligan gardeners, fixing a benchmark of the mid 1800s, set out to recreate the Victorian vegetable garden, selecting plants on the basis of taste and flavour and growing them without either the supposed benefits of modern pesticides, herbicides or fertilisers, or the conventional garden poisons of the Victorian age such as nicotine, arsenic and red lead. Eventually Heligan was supplying its own restaurant and, with a vegetable box scheme, the local neighbourhood with produce from the kitchen garden.

The château at **Villandry** is one of a rash of country houses that lines the Loire valley in France. When a Dr Joachim Carvallo took over the restoration of its formal gardens in the early 1900s, aided on the expenses side by his marriage to a wealthy American heiress, he created one of the world's most decorative vegetable gardens. Designed to be viewed from the high windows of the château or the vine-covered raised walk that surrounded the garden, he arranged for the restoration of Villandry's eighteenth century gardens basing his work on the engravings of French manor gardens from the 1600s by Jacques Androuet du Cerceau.

There was the Jardin d'Ornement designed by a Spanish artist Lozano to symbolise four stages of love, its box hedges enclosing plants to suggest hearts, flames, masks, fans and dagger blades (for *l'amour tragique*). Then there was the Jardin d'Eau, an ornamental basin connected to a canal and filled with carp. But the glory of the garden was the Jardin Potager, a feature which draws visitors from around the world.

Separated from the Jardin d'Ornement by an avenue of limes, the Jardin Potager was constructed of nine square quarters, each with its own geometric parterre and hedged with low-growing box. Carvallo filled his parterres not with lavish blooms, stately shrubs, or coloured stones as some did, but with every-day French vegetables – over 30,000 of them. Packed together in a maze-like design, there were ruby chard and tomatoes, decorative cabbage and carrots, basil, aubergines and black pimiento. Dr Joachim Carvallo had created the world's most spectacular ornamental potager.

2
Tools, Potting and Pests

THE KITCHEN GARDENER

Children raised on the writings of Beatrix Potter remember the guardian of the garden in *The Tale of Peter Rabbit*. 'Your father had an accident there; he was put in a pie by Mrs McGregor,' warns Peter Rabbit's mother at the start of the story. The young rabbit comes face to face with the curmudgeonly Mr McGregor after the rabbit ate 'lettuces, and some French beans, and then he ate some radishes; and then, feeling rather sick, he went to look for some parsley'. At one point the bearded Mr McGregor endeavours to stamp Peter Rabbit to death.

In the post war years of World War Two an equally sanguine figure featured in an instructional cartoon column in the *Sunday Express*. This was Adam the Gardener, who, like Mr McGregor, had about him an almost detectable smell of stale pipe smoke, charity shop clothes and underwear that received irregular washing. Both vegetable growers, Adam and Mr. McGregor had, as their antecedents, the garden staff of Edwardian England, those churlish servants who would do only what they would do. How did this stereotype arise? And what became of them?

The *hortolanus* or *gardinarius* was a person of status in medieval Europe. The *hortolanus* administered the monastery gardens, overseeing the workers who tilled the soil, planted the garlic and the beans, grafted the fruit stock and ensured that the cloister garden remained free of moss and weeds. The workers were often lay gardeners for, although the early Benedictines and Cistercians exhorted their brethren to till the soil themselves, believing that hard work and abstinence brought one closer to God, they were also very good at recruiting novices from the nobility. The noble brother, however devout, preferred to pay a lay person to do his digging for him. Outside the monastery walls, meanwhile, people looked after their vegetables plots as and when they could in the evenings and, as religious rules permitted, at weekends.

In the 1500s as the prosperity of the Elizabethan age edged across Britain from the south-east to the north and west, Britons spent their new-found money, as they always will, on smart homes and fine gardens in what the landscape historian W.G. Hoskins described as the Great Rebuilding of Britain. We can only assume that women were the mistresses of these gardens: as William Fitzherbert noted in his 1534 *The Book of Husbandrie*: '... the beginning of March ... is time for a wife to make her garden.' Although evidence of the woman's role as the kitchen gardener goes largely unrecorded (apart from occasional accounts of women paid as weeding labourers), common sense suggests that the housewife who managed the household would have kept a close eye on the productive vegetable garden. Early garden authors such as Thomas Tusser – they were all men – suggest that women's work was confined to the flowers, herbs and medicinal plants. Yet in 1617 William Lawson brought out the

Countrie Housewifes Garden giving kitchen garden advice on such matters as the 'Planting, Graffing, and to make Ground good for a rich Orchard', and on the 'Husbandry of Bees, with their several Uses and Annoyances'. A century later Charles Evelyn, son of the garden writer and designer John Evelyn recognised a gap in the market and published his *The Lady's Recreation* which included 'directions for the raising, pruning, and disposing of all lofty vegetables.'

In the early 1800s women gardeners began to gain a higher profile. When Jane Webb, the daughter of a Birmingham engineer, married the prolific garden writer John Loudon, she helped her husband with his books and encyclopedia and wrote a series of books for women gardeners including *Gardening for Ladies* and *The Ladies' Flower-Garden*. She also edited *The Ladies' Companion*, which was founded in 1849. Loudon, twenty-four years her senior, made little concession to the role of the women in the kitchen garden. A labourer's garden, he wrote for example, should be large enough to occupy the man in digging and planting and those of 'the female part of the family' or the 'wife and children in hoeing, weeding and watering'. It echoed the attitude of the times epitomised by the King of Sweden's alleged aside to his wife: 'Madam, I married you to give me children, not to give me advice'.

Times would change. In 1913 women suffragettes attacked the clubby men's world of the garden in their campaign for votes for women by destroying plants in the orchid house at the Royal Botanic Gardens in Kew. Fifteen years earlier the heiress Ellen Willmott (who died penniless after spending her fortune on her gardens), was awarded the coveted Victorian Medal of Honour for her horticultural work. She shared it with 'the rather fat, and rather grumbly' Gertrude Jekyll, who herself managed a substantial kitchen garden at her home in Munstead Wood, Surrey. The description of Miss Jekyll came from another woman gardener who would become one of the most influential voices in gardening, Victoria Sackville-West.

However, although Gertrude Jekyll and Ellen Willmott both had a reputation for hands-on gardening, their most useful gardening tool was the jobbing gardener himself (Ellen Willmott employed over a hundred gardeners at her Warley Place garden in Essex). For two millennia at least, jobbing gardeners who, in the kitchen garden, were the ones 'grubbing weeds from gravel paths' as Rudyard Kipling put it in his poem *The Glory of the Garden* in 1911. Cheap, and good at all those back-breaking jobs such as manuring, digging and weeding the vegetable plot, the jobbing gardener was also the ideal tool for planting out and protecting tender seedlings, and harvesting and storing crops.

Jobbing gardeners, like lighthouse keepers and clergymen, were a curious and sometimes eccentric breed. Too isolated by their livelihood to have formed a trade union movement, their pay traditionally hovered around the agricultural wage. They were often illiterate: Richard Payne Knight, the scholar who made a name for himself when he attacked Capability Brown's landscape style, ran his estate at Downton, Herefordshire with the aid of gardener who 'is an extremely simple laborer. He does not know a letter or a figure.'

When things went wrong in the garden, the jobbing gardener could, and often did, take the blame: 'If those who have private gardens were a little more difficult to please in selecting a gardener, and in the quality of the produce sent to table, the consequences would be an improvement in that produce, and more scientific gardeners,' insisted a haughty Mr Loudon.

However, while most paid gardeners had to be content with their servitude, some, especially in Victorian and Edwardian times, rose through the social ranks to become men of status and influence. When the bachelor gardener William Robinson died in 1935, he left a 360-acre estate, including an acre of kitchen garden, and the Elizabethan manor house of Gravetye in Sussex. He was the wealthiest garden writer of his time yet he had begun his working life as the garden boy at Curraghmore in Ireland. By 21, he had risen to the rank of foreman in charge of the precious glasshouses on an estate in County Laois. Said to have abandoned his hothouse charges in the middle of the night, the windows open and the fires extinguished, after an argument with the owner, Robinson had set off to Dublin to find a new post. It was a good story, if an unlikely one, for he soon found a job with the Royal Botanic Society in London's Regents Park and began contributing articles to *The Gardener's Chronicle*. *The Times* sent him to Paris as their horticultural correspondent and by 1868 he had published his first book, *Gleanings from French Gardens*. The once-poor, apprentice gardener never looked back. He set up a magazine, *The Garden*, in 1875 recruiting that other influential writer, Gertrude Jekyll who would herself edit the magazine at the century's turn in 1899. *The Garden* was sold and merged with *House and Gardens* in 1927, but Robinson had already founded another magazine, *Gardening Illustrated*, aimed at the up and coming suburban and villa gardeners. By 1838 this gardener turned publisher was employing his own army of gardeners when he bought Gravetye Manor. His relations with his gardening staff and head gardener Ernest Markham were said to be good. (When he died his last wish, to be cremated, was fulfilled: he had been an early campaigner for cremation.)

In Robinson's day the gardener's craft was handed down from generation to generation. When the late George Watkins, a former head gardener on a Shropshire estate, started work in the early 1900s, his education was a hand-me-down affair: 'I worked under a very clever gardener, George Crew. He had a wonderful way of teaching. He'd give me some packets of seed then he'd keep an eye on me, like, and I got to grow those seeds on, potting on and that sort of thing. With this coaching, he never did anything without he told me what he was doing and the why and the wherefore.'

As a boy the gardener-to-be would join the house staff as pot washer and apprentice, spending a year or so in the kitchen garden on menial tasks, before moving to spend another year or two on the flower borders. An ambitious young gardener might move on to be a journeyman, settling at one garden to gain experience before moving on to another. In this way he would improve his skills and widen his knowledge until he could apply for his first post as foreman at a large garden, or head gardener at a smaller establishment.

In an era when it was fashionable to keep a fine garden, but unfashionable to rummage around in the soil, the position of head gardener was a potentially prestigious one. Yet for most who maintained the nation's gardens and grew the household's vegetables, their social ranking in the pecking order 'below stairs' was relatively low. And, as George Watkins recalled: 'You had to touch your cap to all these toffs, you see.' The post had its advantages. Watkins again: 'When I was a boy starting in the gardens, gardeners worked until four o'clock on a Saturday, but farmers till five or six. In 1920, 1921, when I was in Yorkshire, I didn't have to work after twelve o'clock on a Saturday. That was strange to me.' When he moved to Shropshire his Saturday afternoons remained garden-free because the local squire for whom he worked had a passion for village cricket. 'Sir Henry Ripley, he'd got a great Daimler tourer that would take the whole team: that was how keen he was on the village team.'

Generally, however, social class dictated that the gardener and his lordship were not seen in society together. While the gardener might carry on undisturbed in the vegetable plot he was expected to keep a low profile in the rest of the garden and remove himself if there were guests about. The kitchen gardener was a necessary nuisance. The mistress of the house had to produce a good table of vegetables and the key to production was her kitchen garden staff: friction between the mistress of the house and the kitchen gardener could have serious consequences. In fiction P.G. Wodehouse's Lord Emsworth was continually frustrated by his sister's head gardener, McAllister. Fact is stranger than fiction: the stubborn jobbing gardener on one large estate in the English Midlands regularly received a tray of young lettuce seedlings from his mistress for planting out. Just as regularly the gardener made sure they caught a late frost or were taken by slugs, while informing his mistress that her plants had failed once again because the local ground was just not good enough for them.

One commentator in the 1800s, John Latouche, condemned such relationships: 'Have you no spirit left that you submit to be dictated to by a servant?' he demanded to know. Occasionally the owner made her displeasure public. Baroness Rolle of Bicton in Devon did so of her head gardener, James Barnes, in the 1860s, telling friends that when he left her service, he had abandoned Bicton in a disordered state. Barnes sued the Honourable Baroness for libel, winning the case in 1869 and receiving the equivalent of two years pay, £200, in compensation.

It seems that the grim Mr. McGregor, the dour Adam and the intractable McAllister owe their reputations to these stern Edwardian and Victorian gardeners.

SPADE, HOE AND HOOK

Not normally a day of special celebration, 1 September is, nevertheless, the feast day of the patron saint of the spade, Saint Fiacre. In the 600s Fiacra left his native Ireland for France where he was welcomed by the Burgundian-born Bishop Faro of Meaux. Faro gave Fiacra a piece of land to found a monastery near what is now Saint-Fiacre-en-Brie. But he imposed one troublesome condition: the monastery could occupy only so much land as could be dug by one man in one day.

Fiacra himself took up the challenge with his trusty spade. When the sun set Fiacre had turned the sod of no less than 9 acres. A hermitage was founded on the site and hermitage it was: women were strictly excluded and, even after Fiacra's death, any that trespassed were said to suffer mysterious misfortunes.

Fiacra was destined for sainthood. His reputation as a gardener and a grower of fine vegetables was eclipsed only by his phenomenal powers for curing haemorrhoids. His chapel and shrine are at Meaux and his emblem is, of course, the spade. (His memory was also enshrined by Parisian cab drivers. When the four-wheeled cabs first appeared for hire in the French capital close by the Hôtel Saint-Fiacre, they were known as *fiacre*.)

Irish links with the spade have continued down the ages. Gangs of Irish 'inland navigators' or navvies formed the backbone of the men who built Britain's railways and canals. They worked with the same basic hand tool as Saint Fiacre, although it was hand crafted to their own designs. A century ago the craft had developed into one of local distinctiveness as the men of the Ulster spade mills made different spades to meet the specific demands of local soils and local traditions. They manufactured more than a hundred different types from the thin, bladed 'loys' of the south and west of Ireland to the dependable two-shouldered Ulster digging spade. There were mud spades and drain spades, trench spades and *slanes* for cutting peat, each fitted with an ash handle.

The suggestion that designs also catered for the Irish gardener who traditionally dug the kitchen garden with his right foot, and the Englishman who used his left, are spurious, however. Spades were often made with a footrest on either the left, or the right side, although in later years they were made with a footrest on either side. The suggestion that a Catholic man dug with the left or the 'wrong' foot was a term of abuse, perhaps implying that the left-footed digger was a bog-dwelling peasant who used an old-fashioned spade.

The forerunner of the spade was a very down to earth, peasant implement, the mattock or, in Ireland, the *matóg*. The mattock was spade, hoe, trencher and root digger all rolled into one. A close relative of the adze, the housebuilder's axe used to fashion green and unseasoned oak into housebeams, and the butcher's pole axe, the mattock had a broad blade at the one end and a blunt point at the other. As metal technology improved, the garden fork, hand trowel, four-pronged fork and hoe, tended to push the mattock to the back of the tool shed (although it still serves rural communities across the globe).

Weeding might be done with a hoe or a forked stick and a hook 'ground sharpe both behind and before' as suggested by William Fitzherbert in *The Book of Husbandrie* while the thorny problem of clearing virgin ground was solved with a hook or bill hook. The design of the hook, like that of any other tool prior to the Industrial Revolution, varied from region to region, even from parish to parish. In England alone more than twenty-five designs have been recorded for hedge making, pruning and cutting back, and harvesting stakes and poles from the woods: 'by hook and by crook' was a legal term for working the manor woods.

The bill hook's smaller brother, the sickle, was a harvesting tool, handy for topping large quantities of carrot or beet before they were put to store in sand or peat, and clearing paths and around fruit trees. Down the years a favourite sickle would come to resemble the cusp of a new moon with its thin, razor-edged blade. The bill hook's big brother, the scythe, came into its own in the autumn for mowing the long meadow or orchard grass. In times of trouble and political unrest such as the 1381 Peasants' Revolt all four – mattock, scythe, sickle and hook – were appropriated from the tool store and born as lethal weapons for close combat fighting. (History would repeat itself when the garden tool shed was once again raided in World War Two by weaponless British Home Guardsmen preparing for the anticipated invasion of their country by Nazi Germany.)

A basic tool set illustrated by John Evelyn in the 1660s shows a conventional range of tools including wooden sieves for sifting potting soil, seed sowing boxes, dibbers, and wooden rakes lined with timber teeth. Those 'wedge(d) with oke' were the superior sort. If Evelyn were to journey forward in time for three and half centuries he might be amused to find the hoe, rake, hook and shears of his age still in use although he would be confounded by the quantity of wasted plastics employed in the garden.

The start of Queen Victoria's reign marked the start of mass marketing in the kitchen garden tool trade. During her sixty-four-year tenure – she died in 1901 – she ruled a quarter of the globe and one in four of every person on it. Her servants gardened in far flung corners of the empire: 'Your Le Floral is the most remarkable stuff,' wrote Sergeant-Major J. Binns of Pachmarhi, Central Provinces, East India to Sutton's seeds ('seedsmen to His Imperial Majesty the German Emperor') in 1837, a company, which, in common with the garden tool makers, offered 'carriage paid to all the principal ports in England when orders amount to 60s'.

Victoria's long reign would witness the transformation of the kitchen garden and the tools that turned it. In 1851 her husband Prince Albert organised The Great Exhibition at the Crystal Palace in London. More than 100,000 exhibits were displayed including the very latest in kitchen garden technology. One gardener who attended the Great Exhibition, but then refused to go inside because he disapproved of the 'ugly' exhibits was the 18-year-old William Morris. He thought the Exhibition had been hijacked by the nation's industrialists and used as a vehicle to promote mass production. (Morris' Arts and Crafts movement would one day spread to garden design, espousing the cause of the Romantic medieval garden and its handsome hand tools.)

Six million attended the Exhibition and they had money to spend. Their tool stores were soon filled with every conceivable horticultural device. Sutton, for example, could offer a choice of three dozen garden penknives including a special asparagus knife, Ladies budding Knife, Pruning Knife and Saw ('Superior') and Knife with two blades and botanical lens; there were seven different spades and twenty-two different hoes; five 'Improved Garden Engines' (or wheeled water barrels) and eight wheelbarrows with a choice of wooden or iron wheels; and no less than twenty-eight different carts for carrying manure.

Two world wars later, and with no labour force to use the tools, tool sheds filled with dusty relics. Some were profitably tidied away with the latest American invention, the shadowboard, which offered a proper place for every tool. Most, however, were thrown on the scrap heap as steel and plastic usurped the old iron and ash- or hickory-handled tools. In the post war period new tools for the kitchen garden were designed to help the single-handed owner-gardener manage alone. The ubiquitous mechanical tiller, which took American kitchen gardens by storm, was invented by a Swiss gardener and based on his observations of a dog digging for a bone. Meanwhile wheeled hoes and powered ploughs, steel wheelbarrows and chain saws, strimmers and chuntering motor mowers flooded the market – Sunday mornings would never be quiet again.

Innovations included hopeless failures like the hand weeding glove of 1965, which dripped with weed killer and was used to stroke offending weeds to death, and spectacular successes like the Flymo, the hover mowing machine that glided over grassy paths between the vegetable beds, or the Gro-bag that encouraged even those with no garden to grow a small crop of vegetables. Nevertheless, certain hand kitchen garden hand tools did stand the test of time. They included the hand-trowel, the French secateurs introduced by the garden writer William Robinson and, in France at least, the Opinel penknife.

Jo Opinel lived in the Savoy region of France and created his classic knife in 1890. With its hardened steel blade, which could be locked in place by a steel ring, and its palm-shaped wooden handle, the Opinel came in twelve different sizes, each carrying the trademark symbol of a crowned hand. (The Opinel owner was expected to drill a hole in the handle himself and run a cord through so that it could hang from his trouser belt.) While Pablo Picasso was said to have used his favourite Opinel to carve small sculptures, one alpinist owed his own life to his trusty Opinel: buried in an avalanche in 1959, Pierre Paquet used his Opinel to cut a way out of his snow tomb. But for the most part the Opinel served the French kitchen gardeners for a century of slicing onions, trimming bean sticks and cutting raffia. William Morris would have approved.

HOW BIG IS MY GARDEN?

Measurement is an essential tool in the vegetable garden. It always was. Early Frankish law dictated that, for the purposes of legal compensation, an orchard had to consist of at least twelve trees in an enclosure 60ft by 80ft. 'The Brazil beet requires eighteen inches; and the plants a foot and a half asunder for the crop sown in April,' declared the garden writer Shirley Hibberd in the late 1800s. 'Cabbage. Sow thinly 1 inch deep. As soon as the plants have made four or five leaves they should be planted out from 24 inches apart,' advised one post war garden guide.

The desire for accuracy in the vegetable beds can become an obsession (and we will temporarily abandon the metric system to better appreciate it). With her husband away fighting, this Second World War-time West Midlands housewife was determined to dig for victory to supplement her rations. 'I dug up the front lawn and learned to grow vegetables from my neighbour. He was an old man and he always used a tape measure not only between the rows and between the plants too.' This veteran gardener relied on the Imperial system, in use in Britain for 600 years until the British Parliament voted to go metric in 1963.

The principal unit of measurement has always been the human body – horses are still measured in hands, people still pace out their plots and sow with a 'pinch' of seeds. A foot, a step and an arm span were useful measures in the Middle Ages when Henry I legalised his 'imperial' measure of the foot and the yard (3ft), which was based on the distance between the tip of the Royal nose and the thumb of his outstretched arm. Before he died in 1135, an Iron Yard of Our Lord King was lodged in London and exact copies, cast in bronze or brass, were delivered throughout the kingdom.

Five thousand years ago the boundaries surrounding the farms and vegetable gardens along the river Nile were regularly washed away and the Egyptians used a rope of 100 cubits, the cubits marked off with knots, to re-establish their garden boundaries. The Royal Cubit was cast from a block of black granite against which every cubit measuring stick was checked for accuracy. The cubit could be subdivided into twenty-eight 'digits' and the construction of the pyramids demonstrates the success of their system.

Two thousand two hundred years ago the first Emperor of China, Shih Hung Tio, fixed a standard measure of length, a *chih*. It was 250mm long and based on the distance between the pulse and the base of the thumb. The *chang* was approximately 3m long.

When the centre of power in the Middle East swung away from Egypt towards the Mediterranean it was the turn of the Greeks who, still using a variant on the finger, adapted the Egyptian cubit to equal twenty-four fingers. They made their basic unit of length one foot or sixteen fingers. When it was the Roman's turn to set a worldwide standard, they too used the foot (*pes*), but sub divided it into the *uncia* or twelfth, the origin of our inch. Longer lengths were measured as a pace, which was two steps, one with the left foot, one with the right, and a thousand paces made a *mille*, or a mile.

A foot, a step or an arm-span were still useful garden measures in the Middle Ages. While merchants measured their spun wool in *ells*, the distance between the elbow and the fingertip, and the Vikings measured a fathom as so many lengths of a sailor's arm, the mediaeval vegetable garden was measured in feet. A standard size, measured with an 84ft cord on a triangulation of 3: 4: 5 (21ft, 28ft and 35ft) produced a 28ft-long and 21ft-wide vegetable plot. The plot could be divided into four or five strips, narrow enough to allow the bed to be cultivated without the gardener walking across it and compacting the soil. 'Beds should be so contrived that the hands of those who weed them may easily reach the middle of their breadth, so that those who are weeding may not be forced to tread on seedlings, to the help of which let the paths be of such a width (as a man's foot) that they may weed first one half and then the other half of the bed,' advised Thomas Hill very sensibly in 1577.

Larger garden areas occurred in the village 'clos' (in Scandinavian the 'toft') a strip of ground at the rear of the cottage, measuring between 30ft and 60ft wide and 200ft to 600ft long. Although part of the patch would be put down to pasture and orchard and part devoted to those wonder materials of the medieval age, flax and hemp, a significant area would be dug by foot ready for planting the plants or *worts*. The furlong, an eighth of a mile and based on the distance a horse could plough without needing to pause for a rest, was more of an agricultural measure, but the acre, representing a patch of ground which a team of oxen could plough in a day, was, and still is, used for larger gardens. The acre measured 4840 square yards and could be sub divided into 160 *perches*, from the Latin pole or staff. Measuring the feet of the first sixteen parishioners leaving the church on a Sunday was judged a sound method of establishing a perch.

Apart from the addition of the 22-yard-long 'chain' introduced by Edmund Gunter (1581–1626), the British astronomer and mathematician whose surveyor's chain became an official measure of length across the British empire, the Imperial system served the vegetable gardeners of England unchallenged until 1791. Then in post-revolutionary France, a committee of the French Academy of Sciences defined a new, revolutionary unit of measurement, the metre, so called after the Greek word, *metron*, or measure. The committee based the system on multiples of ten and the basic unit, the metre, on one-ten-millionth of the distance between the Equator and the North Pole. Unable to actually measure that distance, two French engineers calculated it after measuring the more manageable distance between Dunkirk and Barcelona.

When the new metric system was adopted, the Gallic equivalent of the Egyptian's granite cubit, made of a platinum and iridium alloy, was sent to the Bureau International des Poids et Mesures at Sèvres near Paris. Plaques showing the standard measure were put up in public places across France. The metric system was introduced to the United States over a century ago, but largely ignored by gardeners. It was legally brought in to the UK in the 1970s as part of Britain joining the European Union, but there was a marked reluctance amongst gardeners to use anything other than King Henry's imperial standard. And despite the advent of the motor car, the aeroplane and the computer, allotment dimensions continued to be based on the measurements of the Middle Ages: section 22 of the Allotments Act 1922 describes an allotment garden as 'not exceeding forty poles in extent'.

UNDER GLASS

In some parts of the Dutch lowlands the sight of naked soil is a rarity. Instead, a sea of glass covers the polders and protects acres of vegetables ripening with all the advantages of free solar power. Now, in the new, mechanised age of gardening, the Dutch glasshouses hum with the computers that control the hydroponically grown tomatoes and cucumber plants. Not for nothing were glass-covered vegetable frames, or Dutch lights, so named.

Just under four centuries ago John Evelyn explained his own method of harnessing natural energy to grow plants when he delivered his Philosophical Discourse on Earth to the Royal Society, an organisation established by Charles II and devoted to promoting the arts and sciences. Evelyn explained how forcing pits, deep enough for a man to stand in, could be filled with steaming hot dung. Plants grown on in portable wooden trays over the pits positively thrived with this natural bottom heat. Shirley Hibberd in his *Profitable Gardening* gave the forcing pit his vote: 'In times gone by there was nothing better than the hot house frame or pit, heated with leaves and stable manure, and in skilful hands there was generally no difficulty in obtaining plenty of fruit'. But, he warned, 'the dung-frame was very uncertain of productiveness.'

Evelyn and his Discourse helped to promote the 'green house' and the 'conservatory', both places where gardeners could conserve their green plants over winter. Early experimenters used wood, stone and brick to create greenhouses, but by 1697 the Duke of Devonshire had one of the first glass greenhouses built at Chatsworth. Designers knew that ventilation was vital, that the reflective quality of whitewashed walls raised the temperature inside, and that a glass roof set at a slope of precisely 52 degrees would maximise the effects of the sun, which, at midday, struck the glass at right angles.

Technical developments were spurred on by a mania for growing tender plants especially the pine or pineapple, by the repeal of a tax on glass in the 1840s and by nations competing to build the most spectacular winter gardens. The 90m-long Jardin d'Hiver in Paris' Champs Elysées rose up almost three stories high in 1847 while a vine house at Buffalo in the US housed over 200 vines in its 210m length. However, the greenhouse and the conservatory went in opposite directions especially after Joseph Paxton built his prestigious Crystal Palace in 1851: the conservatory became an aspirational addition to the Victorian villa while the greenhouse was turned into an essential tool to service the Victorian table.

Shirley Hibberd regarded the greenhouse as a thing of beauty. 'A houseful of melons or cucumbers, showing a rich screen of foliage between the eye and the sun, and the fruits hanging below it, as they would naturally if the plants were twining among the trees of their native soils, is one of the finest sights in the whole range of horticultural exhibitions.'

Technical advances in glass-making powered the development of the greenhouse. In the early 1800s broad or cylinder glass was blown into a cylinder and then opened out flat to be cut into sheets. Plate glass, where molten glass was poured out onto a casting table and then laboriously ground and polished smooth, was introduced in the late 1800s. Both were too expensive for horticultural use. The alternative was crown glass, which was spun into a large disc and then cut into squares and diamonds, the bull's eye centre being thrown back into the furnace. John Loudon declared that 'economy, as to the quality of glass' was self-defeating and would result in 'the sickly pale etiolated appearance of plants more painful than agreeable to the eye of any who take an interest in the vegetable kingdom'. When Sir Joseph Paxton designed a cast iron glazing bar with a rainwater channel on the upper side and a condensation channel on the inner face (freely taken from nature – the Paxton gutter was modelled on the leaf of the giant water lily) it opened the floodgates on a frenzy of greenhouse building. There were great, double span cucumber houses and meloneries, modest plant preservers, 'lawn' conservatories 'invaluable for the use of Amateurs in the forwarding of ... various seeds', pit frames, lean-to greenhouses and lean-to forcing houses calculated to 'convince all practical minds of the importance and utility of this class of House for Gentlemen, Nurserymen, Market Gardeners, and, in fact, all those who require a cheap, strong House for Forcing, or growing Cucumbers, Tomatoes, Melons, &c, &c', as one Victorian garden catalogue put it.

Outside the glass house gardeners rich and poor took advantage of the cold frame and the French *cloche,* originally a bell-shaped glass (hence its name), to bring on early vegetables or shelter late ones from the autumn frosts. Inside the greenhouse a variety of heating systems were tried out from pits of tan bark (sheets of oak used in the tanning industry), which reached temperatures up to 42 degrees centigrade, to anthracite, charcoal or coke stoves. There were devices for waking the under gardener in the middle of the night should the temperature fall too low; fire alarms, however, were rare and glasshouses frequently burned down.

Using radiant heat from cast iron pipes filled with heated water and laid beneath the vegetable beds had been in use by the 1750s. The concept, according to Ibn Bassal, gardener to the Sultan of Toledo in the eleventh century is at least a thousand years old. Bassal also published useful advice on water supply, soil and its preparation. His detailed instruction for raising early seedlings, for example, involved employing a dung heap of slightly dried mule droppings pepped up with a soupçon of pigeon dung. Seeds were then sown in a compost of dry-dung, sheltered by cabbage leaves, on top of the heap. The natural bottom heat helped the seeds germinate and grow. The heap could maintain its heat for up to five weeks, but it could prove fickle: if the heap was allowed to overheat it cooked, rather than cultivated, the tender young plants.

Eventually the safer system of steam pipes, laid like a conventional central system, took over in the great glasshouses and the concept of a little 'bottom heat' continues today with gardeners germinating their seed in electrically heated propagators.

Like the walled gardens that sheltered them, the great glass houses eventually slipped into decline as the cost of fuel and labour made them uneconomical. But in the country homes of the 1920s the greenhouse still had a role to play as Shropshire head gardener George Watkins remembered. 'Between the front of the house and the servants' quarters at the back, you had the old green baize door. There's a bell there to ring madam. So you'd go in about ten o'clock in the morning to meet the lady of the house and discuss what vegetables she'd like. You got to try and get about three vegetables a day and you couldn't put the same three vegetables in on the run so you got to get so many varieties to follow on all the year round.

'There was a big conservatory and a heated greenhouse. Heating was so cheap in those days a truck-load of anthracite would be enough to keep you going for the winter. In the conservatory side was vines, then you got to grow carnations, chrysanths, cinerarias, and cyclamen for the lady. Off that again you'd got a plant house where you forced potatoes and beans and tomatoes and cucumbers and anything like that. We used to force dwarf beans, salsify, carrots, beetroots and celeriac — you name it, we got it.'

THE POTTING SHED

The potting shed ('perhaps originally a sloping roof or pent-house to *shed* off the rain,' offers the New Gresham English Dictionary) was an essential item in the vegetable garden. Home to an assortment of broken tools waiting (in vain) to be mended, cropping plans and seed catalogues, old kitchen scales for weighing prize vegetables and a patched-up chair or two, the potting shed was also a wet weather sanctuary. It was largely an invention of the Victorian gardening boom although such places were not unknown in Roman times: archaeologists investigating the remains of a smart Roman palace at Fishbourne in the south of England also found and restored the owner's potting shed.

From then until the Middle Ages, the division between the ornamental garden and the kitchen garden was vague. While monastic designers created clear boundaries between cloister garden, cellarer's garden and orchard, the yeoman's wife who lived nearby would be content to mix a rose or two among her coleworts and peas. (The damask rose, for example, brought back to England by returning Crusaders, was a useful 'first aid' flower, regularly used to treat coughs, colds, eye infections and, according to John Gerard, 'staunch bleedings'). As garden fashions developed, however, the kitchen garden of the 1700s and 1800s was banished to the back of the house, away from the fine flower borders and hand clipped lawns.

Out of sight was not out of mind and enthusiastic amateurs like the Reverend Gilbert White (1720–1793, the author of the *Natural Histories and Antiquities of Selbourne*) would certainly have shepherded guests around his vegetable patch so that they might share his pride in the 'four rows of marrow-fat pease' or his concerns with the vagaries of the weather: 'Sowed a crop of carrots, parsneps, beets, radishes, lettuce, Leeks, Onions; a small crop of Salsafy; red Cabbage-seed, Dutch parsley & Chardoons,' he recorded in his *Garden Kalendar*. 'There had been a glut of wet for five weeks, & the Ground was rather too moist; but worked pretty well.' A century later quiet pride is evident in the letters of vegetable growers, composed perhaps in a well-appointed potting shed, to the seed companies. One gardener declared his 'Dean's Early Prolific cucumber 'perfect in form and very solid' and Mr. William Morton of Shepton Mallet felt compelled to put pen to paper about 'your Wordsley Wonder Pea. I have had in many cases pods with 13 Peas in a pod, and (in one instance only) the, to me, unparalleled number of 14 in a pod.'

The garden catalogues, which from the mid 1800s lured in the unwary with promises of dream crops, also marketed architectural and garden ornaments designed to tempt admiring friends into the kitchen garden. There were fountains for the dipping ponds, sundials, dove cots and bee hives for the walled garden, and follies, glasshouses and rustic summer houses. There were also potting sheds. A 'villa gardener', for example, could spend a profitable Saturday afternoon reconstructing his Portable Hexagon Summer-House (£22) that 'can easily be put together by two persons in one hour'. If he chose to, he could specify one of William Cooper's 'Tenant's Fixtures. This house is made in sections and can easily be put together or taken down and removed'. In large Victorian walled gardens the number of outhouses and sheds might run into double figures with its potting shed, garden office, seed store, bothy for the water boy and tool shed.

Various authorities have advised on the contents of the perfect potting shed. That belonging to 'Mr Beck, of Isleworth, described in the November 1843 edition of the *Gardener's Chronicle*, for example, offered benches for potting and display, 'a large water tub, running on castors, which may be pushed under the bench, out of the way,' a boiler, fruit loft, containers for peat, sand, crocks, a tool and paint cupboard, and a row of bins that enabled Mr Beck, or his gardener, 'to keep all his composts and potting materials distinct, and always ready, so that there is no time lost in hunting after this or that, and the place never needs to be unneat.'

Helena Rutherfurd Ely added 'garden sticks' to the contents of her shed. Once described as the American Gertrude Jekyll, Ely, author of the popular *A Woman's Handy Garden* 1903, suggested keeping the canes 'on hand in barrels', condition 'unpainted: the men can paint them on rainy days.' Her potting shed at Meadowburn Farm, New Jersey also held her own tools: 'On a particular shelf in my tool-room I keep my private trowel and flower scissors, to which are attached long red ribbons as a warning of "Hands off!" to others.'

The garden shed famously served the literary needs of various writers including Dylan Thomas, Roald Dahl and Louis de Bernières while the digital age launched a host of innovative and expensive pods, studios, cabins and huts to cater for a new breed of home worker. But the craft of creative shed making, or its smarter sister the summer house, really belongs on the allotment. From store-bought tool stores to creative day rooms made with the contents of the neighbourhood skip, allotment sheds represent the apotheosis of the wet weather retreat. Those on Nottingham's oldest allotment site, Hunger Hill, even became a place of deaths – not so unusual – and births. In *The Allotment* (1988) authors David Crouch and Colin Ward relate how, during the home-hungry days of the early 1900s, people lived in some of its brick-built summerhouse. One woman, born on site, went on to raise a family of eight there.

Hunger Hill Plot holder Eric Kirten gave me a conducted tour of his brick-built shed with its recycled planks, old doors and recycled windows. A calendar chosen for its buxom subject rather than the relevant year beamed down on the comfortably chaotic interior warmed by a stove fuelled on cut-up wooden window frames. A wonky bench was littered with garden catalogues, seedlings in yoghurt pots and spilled trays of potting compost. 'It's a place of retreat,' explained Eric.

Pest Control

Once upon a time people grew vegetables to stave off starvation. That once-upon-a-time has covered some of the bleakest periods in European history from the Black Death to two world wars. In the new millennium however, many people returned to growing vegetables in the kitchen garden to avoid poisoning their families. In 2002 one survey estimated that 40% of shop-bought vegetables and fruit contained pesticides residues. Fifteen years later the British government's own scientists traced pesticide residues on over half the lettuces, potatoes, apples, radishes, and courgettes tested (Expert Committee on Pesticide Residue in Food, 2015, DEFRA, 2016). They concluded that the samples, although 'above reporting level', were 'not expected to have an effect on health.' Vegetable growers such as Jude Cooper, a Hay-on-Wye allotment holder for over thirty years, was not taking any risks: 'Growing our own vegetables is a form of rest and relaxation and there's a great spirit of camaraderie on the allotments. But above all I can eat what I know – and I know what I grow is free of potentially carcinogenic pesticides.'

A century ago some of the more powerful pesticides used to boost productivity came from natural sources as former head gardener Keith Ruck recalled: 'Nicotine was our main thing for all insecticides and green sulphur for fungi diseases. You bought nicotine liquid from the chemist or you bought nicotine shreds for fumigating the greenhouses. These were tobacco leaves cut up and soaked with nicotine to make them extra deadly. You'd put six heaps in the conservatory and light them. By the time you got to light the last it would be getting a bit strong in there.'

Outside the glasshouse the garden writer Shirley Hibberd advocated a drenching of 'laurel water' to eradicate caterpillars from the brassica tribe. It was a dubious solution: the poisonous laurel (*laurus nobilis*) produced hydrocyanic acid, the same chemical used in the Nazi extermination camps during World War Two. A safer alternative was 'hand-picking – very effectual and not so endless a job as it may appear' or loosing a 'brood of young ducks – the best vermin destroyer' – to clean up the cabbage patch. To protect against club root the Victorian Hibberd suggested dipping the roots of brassica seedlings in a puddle of soot and lime. A century later, gardeners had switched to using the potent disinfectant patented by London chemist John Jeyes in 1877.

According to John Loudon the garden's worst pests were 'the human enemies ... such as break in secretly to steal clandestinely'. He recommended that 'the dog is most effectual', but also considered 'man-traps, spring-guns, and alarums ... have considerable influence'. As with one commentator in the Middle Ages who declared 'wormes that ... waster my herbes, I dash them to death', Loudon too waged war on the friendly worm insisting on 'gathering by hand all worms, snails, slugs, grubs, and other insects, as soon as they appear.'

Poisonous laurel leaves, dried, lit and allowed to smoulder, were once again employed to deal with white- and greenfly; home-made concoctions composed of camphor, soft soap, sulphur and turpentine killed off mealy bugs and soft scale insects; and other plant-based powders and sprays derived from derris, tobacco, hellebore, pyrethrum and quassia were directed at the rest of the insect world. Arsenic was added to the list of poisons used against pests both inside and outside the garden: one Welsh solicitor, Major Herbert Armstrong, was hanged in 1922 for poisoning his wife with arsenic intended for the garden.

Avaricious birds were kept at bay by various means including coating seeds in toxic red lead paint and mounting a scarecrow on the vegetable patch. The traditional gibbet hung with a dead bird would evolve into the cheery mannequin dressed in charity shop clothes, yet the figure of the German *Vogelscheuche* and its Scottish equivalent, the *tattie bogle,* had classical roots. While the Roman Columella (4 CE–70 CE) referred to 'night flying birds on crosses' in his twelve volume *De re rustica*, an earlier poet, Albius Tibullus (d. 19 BCE), championed 'red Priapus [to] be on guard in fruitful gardens so his vicious scythe may scare off birds.' (*Book One Poems*). The sinister figure of the roaming scarecrow has frightened us ever since, especially the chilling representation of Dr Syn, created by writer Russel Thorndyke in his 1915 novel *Dr Syn: A Tale of the Romney Marsh*.

The chemical war, meanwhile, continued. While mothballs, nicotine sprays and pyrethrum entered the human food chain as they were routinely applied to vegetables, the tobacco industry came up with the nicotine-based Black Leaf 40 'an effective and economical insecticide for Plants, Animals, Poultry.' It was eventually banned, but by then a whole chemical armoury, developed for commercial market gardeners and vegetable farmers, had filtered down to the back yard gardener. The carnage in the kitchen garden continued through the 1900s although there were some milder alternatives. Britain's Ministry of Agriculture, for example, recommended derris dust as being especially effective with flea beetle. For those who felt uneasy about chemical killing there was a mechanical aid available – the greased flea beetle wheel. This home-made device consisted of a circle of cardboard, pinned to a cane and plastered with the thick grease normally reserved to lubricate the moving parts on the family's Vauxhall Victor. The theory was sound: as the gardener pushed the greased unicycle along the row of affected beetroot the alarmed flea beetle leapt, as only fleas do, struck the card and stuck fast. (I tried it as a jobbing gardener in the early 1970s. It was a failure.)

It was left to the British garden writer Stuart Dudley ('the only good weed is a dead weed') to reflect the general view of the post-war vegetable grower. 'Let it not be said in this jet age of today that the gardeners of England are fighting the Weed War of today with the weapons of Napoleon,' he wrote in *Taking the Ache out of Gardening:* 'Our back-room boys have provided the wherewithal to blot out the whole of the plant and insect kingdom – let us use them with due circumspection.' The implication was clear: the boffins must know what they were doing and the gardener should carry on with the battle, albeit with care.

By the 1960s, there were clear signs that horticultural and agricultural chemical warfare was damaging the environment. The warnings were, for the most part, ignored: sixty years later the British Trust for Ornithology reported 'the UK's wild bird indicator from 1970 to 2022 clearly demonstrates that overall, birds of wetlands, woodland, uplands and especially farmland, have shown marked declines over the past decades.' The declines, exacerbated by habitat destruction and climate change included the skylark (60%) and curlew (49%). And yet in the 1960s small holder John Seymour was advising gardeners to take a holistic and essentially benevolent approach to growing vegetables. In *The Complete Book of Self Sufficiency* (1973), a practical guide to the recurring, utopian dream of the back-to-the-landers, he suggested the sensitive gardener would 'always get pests and diseases but they will not reach serious proportions. The true homesteader will seek to husband his land, not exploit it,' he wrote. 'He will realize that if he interferes with the chain of life (of which he is a part) he does so at his peril, for he cannot avoid disturbing a natural balance.'

MR HENRY DOUBLEDAY'S SOLUTION

Two new terms entered the common vocabulary of the 1970s, expressions that would have made little sense a decade earlier: moon landing and organic gardening. The former celebrated the fact that an American astronaut stepped out of a spaceship and walked on the moon in 1972. The latter was a response to the way that the average vegetable garden had come to resemble the lunar surface: flowers had been removed from the vegetable patch; garden machines were reducing every nook and corner to a barren sward; and overzealous applications of pesticides and herbicides had left the vegetable plot as regimentally tidy as a military parade on Red Square.

It led the economist Ernst Schumacher, author of *Small is Beautiful* (1973) and a keen gardener, to warn that gardeners were over dependent on machinery: 'People cannot really do anything for themselves,' he declared in the introduction to Seymour's *The Complete Book of Self Sufficiency*. Seymour's own practical advice with its alluring promise of off-grid, pastoral harmony had been dismissed as a 'pipe dream of sweet country life' by Nick Saunders in his *Alternative England and Wales* (1975): 'in reality you have to work harder to produce your own food than you would by earning wages to buy it'. But Saunders did concede that those who grew their own did enjoy 'better quality food and enormously more satisfaction.' It was this, the pleasure principle behind grow-your-own, that produced the most radical change in kitchen gardening since the Dig for Victory campaign: the switch to organics.

The organic notion – that you treat the earth with respect, reap better crops, and somehow improve your mental health by ditching harmful fertilisers, herbicides and pesticides – had been brewing in the agricultural world for some time. Society girl turned organic farmer, Eve Balfour (1898–1990) had already shown that soil was a biological, living entity, and that constant dressing with artificial fertilisers, gradually decreased its fertility over time. The publication of her bestselling *The Living Soil* saw the founding of the Soil Association in 1943 and influenced the American writer, Rachael Carson. Carson's book, *Silent Spring*, published in 1962, posed the seemingly unlikely scenario of a mute dawn chorus if nations continue to poison the land with artificial fertilisers and pesticides. And yet fifty years on, British ornithologists were listening out with despair for the diminishing call of the once common cuckoo, lapwing, nightingale and curlew.

Taking the organic approach into the kitchen garden became the mission for the garden columnist Lawrence D. Hills (1911–1990) who explained in *Grow Your Own* (1971) that he was 'not concerned with argument, philosophy or generalizations but with the methods old and new that make it possible to grow better produce than could be grown in any chemicals-fed garden.' In the dictionaries of the 1930s the word organic merely meant 'pertaining to the animal and vegetable worlds; forming a whole with a systematic arrangement of parts.' In the 1960s, as Hills explained, it was to be invested with a new and potent meaning: an organic gardener would be one who had given up chemical fertilisers, pesticides and herbicides. 'Some (gardeners) change on ethical grounds to stop pollution harmful to birds, bees and men, others to save money, since it is easy even at today's vegetable prices to spend more on chemicals that you save when growing your own food,' he wrote in 1977.

With chemical fertilisers being widely promoted ('Vigoro-Amos-phos – goes to work at once. Regardless of the poorness of soil,' as one US advert boasted in the 1960s) Hills, looking for a natural alternative, declared for a plant from the borage family, comfrey, having stumbled on the unpublished research of an impoverished nineteenth century Quaker from Essex, Henry Doubleday. In the 1870s Doubleday, who ran a small gum factory, had experienced difficulties sourcing his usual gum arabic. When he heard that prickly comfrey (*Symphytum asperum*), a native of the Caucasus, was reputed to contain much 'mucilaginous matter', he wrote to the gardener at the palace of St. Petersburg in Russia requesting some plants. Doubleday hoped to extract a glue from the comfrey for use on postage stamps. The gardener sent Russian comfrey (*Symphytum X uplandicum*) by mistake. A natural hybrid, the Russian comfrey was no use for gum, but Doubleday, who was also a smallholder, realised its potential as a fodder crop. He set out to improve the variety by selecting the best plants with the highest yields in the hope that the free fertility offered by comfrey might stave off famine in the future: the social unrest and distress caused by the 1850s Irish potato famine were still resounding around Britain.

Since most of Doubleday's notes had been lost, apparently destroyed after he died, Hills began his own comfrey trials on an acre of rented land at Bocking near Braintree in Essex. 'Comfrey,' he wrote in his *Organic Gardening*, 'is so rich in protein ... that it is a kind of instant compost. It has roots that go down 4–8 feet, which is deeper than most fruit trees, but instead of locking up the minerals in the wood where only fire and fungi can release them, it keeps them all in a "current account", as it were, ready for immediate use by crops.'

His best performer for the kitchen garden was Bocking 14 (*Symphytum uplandicum*), 'a semi-sterile hybrid between *Symphytum asperum* from Russia and the wild *Symphytum officinale*, the herbalists' comfrey'. Hills founded an organisation, the Henry Doubleday Research Association, to spread the word and the comfrey. Its networking group of enthusiastic member gardeners grew quickly. By the start of the 1970s, there were 17,000 members sharing their own ideas on organic gardening.

As the organisation expanded two young scientists, Alan and Jackie Gear, responded to an advertisement in *The Times*: 'Young couple wanted to work on an organic research station. Full board. No pay' and joined HDRA. In the 1980s as Lawrence Hills handed the running of the organisation over to the Gears, the couple moved HDRA to its new home, then a run-down, wind-swept 22-acre smallholding near Coventry at Ryton-on-Dunsmore.

Hills died in the 1990s, but not before he had seen HDRA, with a membership of around 30,000, become the largest organic organisation in Europe with the future king of England, the Prince of Wales, as its patron. Ryton was now home to sample organic gardens devoted to ornamental vegetables, different methods of growing vegetables, and a children's vegetable patch. There were other exhibition plots at Yalding in Kent and the Victorian walled kitchen garden at the Jacobean manor house Audley End in Essex, had been restored by HDRA. There was a heritage seed library to rescue old and odd vegetable varieties, and the organisation was supporting farmers in developing countries to grow organic vegetables. It had influenced individuals including broadcaster gardeners Geoff Hamilton and Monty Don, and organisations like the RHS. 'When we began we were just seen as cranks,' Jackie Gear reflected in a YouTube film. Fifty years earlier Hills had predicted in *Grow Your Own:* 'Provided we do not drive our soils too hard, the land will go on feeding us through the sunlit centuries when motoring is but a memory.' HDRA, rebranded as Garden Organic in 2004, had set in motion the most momentous change in kitchen gardening habits in a century.

THE SLUG AND SNAIL WAR

'Sowed a pint more of dwarf kidney beans in the room of those that were devoured by snails,' grumbled Gilbert White in 1759, bemoaning the fact that 2,000 years of pest control had failed to resolve a problem that has vexed gardeners since kitchen gardening began: slugs and snails.

Here, for what it is worth, is the accumulated wisdom of those 2,000 years.

60–65	Lucius Junius Moderatus Columella suggests offering a sacrifice to the plant gods 'with blood and entrails of a sucking whelp'.
Date unknown	Sprinkle ashes 'from the public baths' around sensitive plants.
1000	An Arab gardener in Spain recommends laying cabbage leaves under which slugs and snails shelter at night. In the early morning the gardener can dispose of them.
1400	Dropping slugs in a mix of ashes and unslaked lime.
Date unknown	A Londoner is reported to be keeping four pet seagulls to deal with these 'little beasts injurious to kitchen gardens'.

1571	Kitchen garden paths are watered with an infusion of walnut leaves, salt and crushed shells.
1760	Crushed tobacco leaves are added to the toxic infusion above.
1820	Slugs and snails can be 'annoyed' by scattering caustic substances over them or by watering them with bitter infusions such as vinegar or lime water.
1850	Hand pick them from beneath decaying leaves or haulms laid down as lures.
1870	Quick lime is sprinkled on slugs.
1900	Plants should be encircled with zinc collars.
1920	Slugs are sprinkled with salt.
1930	Surrounding plants with prickly barley straw heads is recommended.
1930s	Ducklings should be let in to the vegetable garden to forage for slugs and snails.
1950	Place heaps of a mixture of metaldehyde and bran or tea leaves around the attacked crop on a warm evening when the soil is moist. Cover the heaps with wood or grass.
1970	Hand collect slugs and snails and deposit them in a bucket filled with creosote-flavoured water.
1977	Lawrence D. Hills unveils the slug trap. 'The traditional soup plate, wide and shallow, sunk level with the ground and filled with a mixture of 1 part of beer to 2 of water, sweetened with 1 dessertspoonful of Barbados sugar to 1 pint of the mixture.' Hills, who also advocated encouraging hedgehogs ('excellent garden-pest controllers'), reassured readers that the watery beer was insufficient to intoxicate any hedgehog which imbibed it.

1980	Metaldehyde slug baits, formed into pellets and scattered around susceptible plants.
1990	Collecting slugs and snails by hand and throwing them over the garden wall. Or transporting them by car to a different neighbourhood – amateur experiments marking snails shells with paint suggested the snail had good homing instincts.
2000	Watering the garden with the microscopic nematode (*Phasmarhabditis hermaphrodita*), a parasitic creature that killed slugs before being, itself, destroyed by a predatory fungus.
2012	Perhaps the most benign advice came from jobbing gardener Rick Guest: 'Each evening I go around collecting them by hand and then I return them to where they belong and where they are happy to live – the compost heap'.

3

Origins and Losses

A VEGETABLE TIMELINE

People have grown vegetables for 8,000 years at least. One theory – and it remains only a theory – supposes that vegetable cultivation was precipitated by the first famine, which was triggered by a world population too large to continue feeding itself on hunting and gathering alone. The natural balance between communities and wilderness had been reached and passed. From then on, the human race would have to grow their own food if they were to survive. Once they had settled and begun to harvest the wild fruits of the neighbourhood, people started to cultivate plants in a sustainable fashion.

If we contrive to represent the last twelve millennia as twelve months of a calendar year, we would find the Natufian people, who lived in the Middle East to the west of the river Euphrates, already gathering their wild cereals in January of that fictitious year. At the other end of the timeline, around 27 December, the United Kingdom would be mourning the death of a keen vegetable grower, Gertrude Jekyll. She died in 1932.

In our mid January or 10,000 BCE (Before Common Era) the ice sheets that had locked down Europe and North America finally began to melt. In the March of our vegetable year the earliest recorded vegetables were growing around Palestine. The early civilisations had settled in the Middle East, building their palaces and pyramids, towns, ports and, of course, kitchen gardens close to the irrigating rivers of the Tigris, Euphrates and Nile.

By mid April, vegetables were being grown around the borders of modern Iran and Iraq. In Crete the kitchen garden was established by May, in China and Mexico by June, and the Indus Valley of eastern India by August, 2500 BCE in real time!

By mid July (3500 BCE) agriculture and its sister horticulture had been carried across the Indus plain by the Indus Valley civilisation. We know more about the visible surface of the moon than we do of this mysterious culture. Archaeologists have uncovered some of its village factories, but scholars are still wrestling with its script and deliberating on whether it should be read from the left or the right. The scholars have established that by 1700 BCE (or early September) the civilisation had collapsed, perhaps because of political instability, a shift in the course of the great Indus river itself, some other natural disaster such as an earthquake, or a combination of all three.

By mid September (1500 BCE) the ancient Egyptians, planting flowers in their vegetable plots, were growing gardens for pleasure as well as purpose. A literary Greek garden 'full of fruits, also sweet figs and bounteous olives' appears in early October in

Homer's Odyssey. Later that month, or around 300 BCE, according to palaeobotanists, there were celery, beet, carrot, brassicas and asparagus being grown in the southern Mediterranean, and peas, vetch, wheat and barley in northern Europe.

The Romans acquired their gardening crafts from the Greeks and by the end of October (100 BCE) the Latin vegetable garden was as highly productive as it was highly advanced. As the empire expanded through Europe they introduced their own favourites including garlic, onion, leeks, lettuce, mustard, parsnip, skirret (a sweet-tasting edible root), turnip and radish. The collapse of the Roman Empire apparently led to the collapse of the kitchen garden, but this may be more due to a lack of documentary evidence than a paucity of vegetable growers. Now we must wait until mid November and the rise of the monastic garden before finding Britons enjoying a decent plate of vegetables again. They were still not described as vegetables: in early medieval times a 'herb' was used to describe any garden plant whether used as a pesticide, a medicine or for the pot. Not until the third week in November (around the year 700) does the word 'vegetable' creep into common use.

Culinary historians are still looking at establishing the genetic continuity between modern and medieval vegetables, but we would recognise many of the edible plants grown in the kitchen garden twelve centuries ago. Skirrets, garlic, plain-leaved parsley and the medieval broad bean, which can be traced back to the horse bean, were all on the menu. The medieval garden burgeoned with self-seeding salad crops such as fat hen and dandelion, the latter still a common enough salad crop. 'My mother used to cover the young dandelion with a dish to blanch them and keep the dogs from peeing on them,' recalls one young woman from Malvern while a French woman from Cholet remembers: 'Grandmother harvested *pissenlit* and served them with a salad dressing. They made you piss.'

Yellow or red onions, sown as seed or planted as sets, were grown along with green onions, that is any small or bull-necked onion eaten fresh rather than lifted and stored. They came under an assortment of names including ascalonia, fissiles, scallion, chibol, clumping winter onions and holeke. Holeke was the ever-ready onion, *Allium cepa var. perufile*, occasionally confused with the Welsh onion which was not Welsh at all, but 'foreign' from the Old German word Welsch or foreign. The true ciboule or spring onion, *Allium fistulosum*, was a later arrival to Europe from Asia in the 1700s, or mid December of our vegetable year.

By early December, the Renaissance kitchen garden in Europe was well advanced. Meanwhile the last of Spain's Moorish leaders, Boabdil (Muhammad XVII), had surrendered the keys to the city of Granada to his Christian conquerors. He left with a tear on his cheek, by the Puerto del Suspiro del Moro, known as the Moor's Last Sigh after the legendary scolding from his mother Aisha: 'You do well to weep like a woman for what you failed to defend like a man.' Boabdil left behind a rich horticultural inheritance, still to be seen in places such as Valencia where the *huertas verduras*, the irrigated gardens, grow hectare upon hectare of vegetables under the gaze of derelict Moorish castles.

By mid December, as Sir Francis Drake claimed California for England, the two-way vegetable traffic between America and Europe had reached fever pitch. For the next ten days, until Christmas Eve, the kitchen gardens of both nations flourished. In 1850 – or shortly after our Christmas Day – the Irish bogland potato crop failed.

Post-Christmas and, apart from a growing frenzy in the kitchen garden during two world wars, the home-grown produce of the kitchen garden steadily diminished under a tidal wave of increasingly processed food. Vesta introduced the first convenience food, a chicken curry, to the UK housewife in 1962 and ultra-processed foods followed. However, by the very end of December or the early 2000s, north Europeans had rediscovered what Mediterranean Europe had known all along: the best tasting vegetables are the ones you grow yourself.

TOP FIVE

THE WORLD'S OLDEST VEGETABLES

1. Pea (7000 BCE)
2. Bean (6500 BCE)
3. Onion (5000 BCE)
4. Lettuce (2500 BCE)
5. Leek (2000 BCE)

Ranked according to seed remains.

OUT OF THE EAST

Today upwards of seventy different vegetables can be grown in the kitchen garden and, until the opening up of the Americas in the sixteenth century, most originated in the Middle East. The story of how they reached Europe's vegetable plots is a long and sometimes confusing one. Take the **globe artichoke** and its apparent sister, the **Jerusalem artichoke**. The globe or 'green' artichoke, *Cynara scolymus*, looks like what it is – an edible thistle. It first came into the kitchen 4,000 years ago when it was cultivated in the Middle East, in the fertile crescent that lay between the Nile and the Indus.

To the Greeks it was *kardos* or *skolumos,* to the Romans *carduus* which is why the Italians still enjoy their *carciofi*. One Roman painter depicted the fertility god, Priapus, on a Pompeian fresco weighing his monumental member on a set of scales against a globe artichoke, presumably a reference to the artichoke's ancient reputation as an aphrodisiac. The English name originates with Arabian name *al-kharshuf*.

The Jerusalem artichoke, *Helianthus tuberosus*, was related neither to Jerusalem nor the globe artichoke. A member of the sunflower family, the Jerusalem artichoke came from what was to be Europe's second richest source of vegetables, the Americas.

The edible part of the *kaishcucpenauk,* as the Algonquian people called it, is the tuber and it was Samuel de Champlain, one-time governor of French Canada, who reported that the *kaishcucpenauk* tasted of artichoke. The confusion was compounded when the appellation Jerusalem was added, either as a corruption of the Italian for sunflower, *girasole,* or of Terneuzen, the Netherlands port north of Ghent, which dispatched artichokes to England in the early 1600s. By 1617 it was reported to be grown by one John Goodyer in Hampshire. The *kaishcucpenauk* originated on the Great Plains of North America where it was cultivated by native Americans, and by the time European settlers arrived it was growing wild from Georgia to Canada. The Pilgrim fathers, however, viewed the Jerusalem artichoke with as much suspicion as the twentieth century allotment holders who referred to it as the 'fartichoke' for its flatulent reputation. John Gerard had no time for the plant either: 'In my judgement, which way soever they be drest or eaten, they are meat more fit for swine, than men.' In fact, the Jerusalem artichoke is very nutritious and a safe vegetable for diabetics.

Asparagus, *Asparagus officinalis,* was another plant brought in from the wilds by the assiduous gardeners of that fertile region around the Nile and the Indus. Two thousand years later its priapic appearance had earned it its lustful, tumescent Greek name *asparagos.* It was introduced to Europe by the Romans (Pliny reportedly bought three giant asparagus heads that weighed around half a kilogram.) The diarist Samuel Pepys, who died in 1703, reported buying 'a bundle of sparrow-grass' in London's Fenchurch Street for one shilling and sixpence, and growers and market traders alike still sometimes refer to it as 'grass'. It was always regarded as a vegetable extravagance: 'The asparaginous class of esculents may be considered as comparatively one of luxury,' wrote Loudon in the 1800s. 'It occupies a large proportion of the gentleman's garden, often an eighth part; but does not enter into that of the cottager.' He recommended the grower devote 'five square poles of ground, planted with 1600 plants' for a yield of 'six to eight score heads daily.'

Some kitchen gardeners find it difficult to grow, but the wild *Asparagus officinalis* proved to be a determined coloniser, making a stand just about anywhere from Morocco to Manchester. As economically important to Venetian traders as their home-blown glass, (farmers around Bassano del Grappa were busy with their asparagus beds in the 1500s) asparagus was taken to the Americas by the early settlers. It made little impact on the American diet however until it was canned and turned into a cheap, but poor substitute for fresh asparagus.

Other vegetables raised in the Nile and Indus region included the beetroot, carrot, celery, pea and turnip. The **beetroot**, *Beta vulgaris,* was growing here 4,000 years ago. While the Greeks ate the leaf of the beet, the Romans enjoyed its swollen red root, which explains why the English ate their 'Roman beet' in Tudor times. In 1597 John Gerard wrote of the 'great red Beete or Romaine Beete': 'the beautiful roote which is to be preferred before the leaves, as well in beautie as in goodnesse.' Given a good feed, he claimed beetroot could grow to 3.5m (12ft). By 1656 the beetroot, now being grown by the gardener and plant hunter John Tradescant the younger, was referred to as the '*beet rave* or beet-radish' from the French *betterave*.

A direct relative of the beetroot, the **mangle**, mangold or manglewurzle, still grown as a prize exhibit at agricultural shows in the UK, started life in the German Rhineland as a chance hybrid between the beetroot and a white-stemmed chard. The great gnarled roots were fed to cattle, but not before they had been lifted and weathered in a clamp long enough for their natural toxins to have leached away.

The **carrot**, *Daucus carota,* was a younger vegetable than the beetroot, but only by a thousand years or so. Unlike the potato it was welcomed into the British kitchen garden of the 1500s: 'Sowe Carrets in your Gardens, and humbly praise God for them, as for a singular and great blessing.' So instructed the aptronymic Richard Gardiner in his 1599 *Profitable Instructions for the Manuring, Sowing and Planting of Kitchen Gardens*. (*Manuring* meant cultivating).

Three and a half centuries later the propaganda character of Dr Carrot was making a contribution to the British war effort. When Britain was plunged into darkness by the night-time blackout in an effort to hide from enemy bombers, the carrot, packed with vitamins which benefited the optical nerves, was a natural aid for those fumbling their way home in the dark. However, the propagandists' claim that the carrot helped the Allied pilots to find their target on night raids was dreamed up as a cover for the advances being made in radar technology.

Traditional red carrots were just one of a rainbow selection of coloured carrots that ranged from scarlet and purple to white and yellow. The Romans referred to them as both *daucus* and *carota*, (which is why Linnaeus accorded them both names), and while Italy's conquering legions almost certainly brought them through Europe, the European tribes of Saxons, Celts, Angles and Vikings seem to have ignored the beneficial carrot for a thousand years. It was left to the Moors to re-introduce the purple carrot from the Middle East in the 900s. The Spanish Moors were growing carrots by the 1100s, the Germans and Dutch by the 1300s, the English by the 1400s and the American Virginians in the 1600s when colonists first sowed the seed there and let the vegetable loose: the carrot went wild and romped off across the continent. The Chinese would eventually become the world's major carrot supplier, (followed by the United States, Ukraine, Uzbekistan and Russia) but it was industrious Dutch gardeners who, in 1720, produced the Long Orange Dutch cultivar, the prototype for most modern varieties.

It was Moorish gardeners who were responsible for developing knobbly celeriac (*Apium graveolens var. rapaceum*), the swollen-rooted vegetable that became such a popular plant in central and eastern Europe. It was developed from wild celery, as was true **celery**, *Apium graveolens*, and was yet another vegetable that emerged from the Indus plains 4,000 years ago. By Roman times there was talk of the little pot herb called *apium* being used to flavour fish, as a garnish in sauces and as a decorative head gear for their champion games players. But it was left to the future generations of Italians to develop their *sedano*, the crisp, thick stalked celery that we eat today. It may have been introduced to northern Europe by an Italian, Giacomo Castelvetro, who, living in exile in England in 1614, described how to grow and prepare it. When it reached America with the early settlers it too bolted into the wild and spread far and wide.

The **pea**, *Pisum sativum*, was another vegetable which originated in the Middle East. Four thousand years later the Greeks were enjoying their *pisoi*. Subsequently the Romans introduced their *pisum* to the rest of Europe. Early peas had coloured flowers and small pods and were grown as a field crop, but gradually the white flowered garden varieties with larger peas were developed. Thomas Tusser in his *Five hundreth pointes of good husbandrie* of 1577 proposed sowings of 'Runcivall peas', the name derived from the large-seeded peas from Roncesvalle Abbey, Navarre 'a town at the foot of the Pyrenees where ... the name [is] applied to anything of a size larger than usual,' explained Tusser. However, the explanation that the 'runcible spoon', with which the Owl and Pussy Cat ate their mince and slices of quince in Edward Lear's nonsense poem, was derived from Runcivall or Roncesvalle peas seems far-fetched. Dried peas were a winter staple and useful source of protein. They could be ground into flour and, mixed with wheat or rye flours, used in bread making, or soaked to soften overnight for a dish of the traditional pease porridge or pease pudding. Eating green, or barely ripe peas, is a luxury enjoyed only by the vegetable grower and eagle-eyed children although courtiers in the grand palace of the Sun King, Louis XIV, were said to have a passion for *petit poi*. The gardener's alternative is the sugar snap, which was developed by crossing the garden pea with the flat-podded, Asian 'snow' pea. And all three are acknowledged as being as good for gut health, as they are low in calories and a tasty way to reduce the risks of heart disease.

Although the pea had been brought into cultivation and improved in the Middle East, it was one of the earliest domesticated plants. Bronze Age families, for example, were eating peas 5,000 years ago. Could it lay claim to be one of the world's first garden vegetables? Three other vegetables cultivated in what was the fertile Middle East could also be considered as odds-on favourites: the lettuce, the onion and the leek.

In the 1800s an Edinburgh doctor was marketing his *Lactucarium*, an 'opium juice' made from lettuce: the name of the lettuce, *Lactuca sativa,* recalls the fact that the Romans too used it as a mild narcotic. Their lettuce exuded a bitter sap or latex which, having similar properties to laudanum, promised a good night's sleep – the name came from the Roman *lactuca* or milk.

The **lettuce**, a relative of the chicory family, was brought into cultivation far earlier than Roman times. Cos or 'Roman' lettuces were pictured on 5,000-year-old Egyptian tomb reliefs (although they earned the term Roman or their French name *laitue romaine* when they were brought to Avignon by the papal court of the 1300s). Theories abound as to why the English should have named the 'cos' lettuce after the Greek island of Kos, but since Kos was the birthplace of the physician Hippocrates it may have been to mark the medicinal qualities of the vegetable. An Italian recipe from 1614 recommended quartering the lettuce, dressing the quarters with oil, salt and pepper and then roasting them over a charcoal grill before eating them sprinkled with orange juice. With butterheads, crispheads and cut-and-come-again varieties there are now as many different lettuces as there are months in the year.

The second contender for the oldest garden vegetable is the **onion**. To 'know your onions' is to know all. The Indian Brahmin knew the onion well enough to avoid it, and anything else 'arising from impurity', all together. The onion, *Allium cepa,* is a member of the lily family which probably originated in the central Asia regions, although no one knows for sure. Spread by traders throughout the world, it was part of the staple diet in Greek and Roman times, the latter, possibly, giving it the name *unio* for singularity.

The **leek**, *Allium porrum,* like the onion a member of the Lily family, may be one of the world's most ancient vegetables, but it is certainly one of the main ingredients in the world's oldest recipe. A 4,000-year-old inscribed Babylonian tablet suggests using crushed leeks to spice up a lamb stew. The Greeks called the leek *prasa,* the Arabs *kurrats* and the Romans, who brought them into northern Europe, *porrum.* Why the Celtic Welsh, who successfully held out against the invading Romans, should have adopted the leek as their national emblem is something of a national mystery, but given their love of song and oration, it may have been associated with the leek's throat-soothing, mucilaginous qualities: the Roman Nero, derided as a *porrophagus* or leek-eater, ate leeks to improve his voice. Since he also invented the art of sycophantic applause, his success may be thrown into question.

OUT OF INDIA

Two important vegetables, the aubergine and the cucumber, came into cultivation from the Indian sub-continent. The Indian **aubergine**, *Solanum melongena*, is a member of the Solanum family along with deadly nightshade, *Atropa belladonna.* The aubergine was not welcomed when first it arrived in England, partly because of its fearsome family connections and partly because it was blamed for a succession of ailments from piles, halitosis and liver obstructions to a poor complexion and, ultimately, leprosy. But, suggested John Parkinson in the 1600s, it was perfectly safe if boiled first in vinegar.

In Sanskrit it was *vatin-gana,* a wind killer, but it was also known as a melongene, Jew's apple, mad apple, brinjal and egg plant (early varieties were small, white, egg-like fruit rather than the deep purple of modern varieties). Its Hindustani name was *bungan* which became the Arabic *al-badingan*. When the Moslems swept through Egypt and north Africa in the 700s and replanted the local vineyards with their own vegetables, they brought it into Spain (the Spanish still call it *berenjena*), Sicily and the Languedoc region of France.

The **cucumber**, *Cucumis sativus,* came out of the foothills of the eastern Himalayas. This runs counter to the claim of William Tyndale who, when he translated the bible in the 1500s (he was strangled and burned as a heretic for his efforts), asserted in the Book of Isaiah that the daughter of Zion lodged 'in a garden of cucumbers'. In the twenty-first century the vegetable was infamously featured on some of the more salacious web sites, but, grown in England as early as the fourteenth century (in the days of the much-married King Henry VIII), the cucumber was regarded as an enemy of lust by the sixteenth century garden author Thomas Hill. He also claimed that a thunderstorm would cause the cucumber to bend. The cucumber was so called after the Old French *cocombre*. However, the 'little wild cucumber' of the West Indies, although related to the cucumber, and better known as the **gherkin**, *Cucumis anguria,* was carried from southwest Africa to the West Indies in the 1600s with the slave trade. It earned its name from the Dutch *augurkje*.

The Roman Emperor Tiberius had a particular passion for the *cucumis* and the Romans created fantastical shaped cucumbers by encasing the young fruits in wood, wicker or clay casts. There was to be none of this nonsense in the Victorian kitchen where the cook insisted upon long, straight fruit, achieved by hanging lantern-like glass cylinders around the growing cucumber.

OUT OF ROME

When the conquering Romans arrived on the shores of Britain in the year 43, they not only introduced their civic buildings, their villas and their roads, but also their ornamental gardens and their favourite vegetables. For example, the wild **cabbage**, *Brassica oleracea,* has uncertain origins although the Greeks, Romans, Moors and Italians were primarily responsible for its spread and it was Romans who brought it to northern Europe along with radishes, parsnips, turnips and carrots. (After the fall of the Roman empire the root crops were largely forgotten and it was left to the wholesome cabbage and onions to fill a hungry gap of 1,000 years until the Renaissance.) A polymorphic plant is one that, chameleon-like, can take on different forms. The cabbage is a polymorphic triumph and there are six main cultivars: non-heading kales, heading cabbages, swollen stemmed kohlrabi, Brussels sprouts, broccoli and cauliflower. But leave them growing together for long enough and all six will cross pollinate and gradually revert to their wild cabbage cousin.

Each of the brassicas seems to have developed as a regional favourite. **Brussel sprouts**, for example, were first recorded in Belgium around 1750, hence the name. 'At Brussels they are sometimes served at table with a sauce composed of vinegar, butter, and nutmeg, poured upon them hot after they have been boiled,' reported an incredulous Loudon. In north-eastern Europe, *choucroute* or *sauerkraut*, made from finely shredded cabbage leaves pickled with juniper berries and sea salt for three weeks in stone crocks, became a favourite. The **cauliflower** was brought into Spain in the 1400s by the Moors and was growing in London a century later. The **broccolis** were always an Italian favourite. The English botanist Philip Miller, from the Chelsea Physic Garden, described it as Italian asparagus in 1724 and it was Italian immigrants who took their beloved broccoli to America (although not until the early 1900s).

Kohlrabi, possibly the vegetable described as a 'Corinthian turnip' by Pliny The Elder, was promoted as a novelty vegetable in Victorian times. Jane Grigson in *The Vegetable Book* of 1978 took a less-said-the-better approach to kohlrabi: 'There are better vegetables than kohlrabi. And worse.' Which may explain why much of the kohlrabi grown in Britain was fed to cattle.

The old English name for the **turnip**, *wort*, belies its ancestry as a member of the brassica family. In Ireland the Gaelic *neip* was an important crop, sown in drills, which ran the length of the field alongside the potato ridges. The seed, sown and weeded by hand, would be dipped in highly toxic red lead to protect it against birds.

The Romans also enjoyed their *pastinaca* **or parsnip**. The Frenchman still enjoys *la panais*, the German his *pastinake*, the Russian his *pasternak* and the Italian his *pastinaca*, since it was the Romans who introduced the parsnip, *Pastinaca sativa*, to these countries. The English linked the French *pasnaie* with the turnip or neep, and John Gerard gave it his qualified support: 'the Parsneps nourish more than do the Turneps or the Carrots, and the nourishment is somewhat thicker; but not faultie nor bad.' The parsnip sweetened in the ground, its starch being converted to sugar by frost action. It was eaten on Ash Wednesday during Lent, cooked to accompany salt cod. Thomas Hill in his *Gardeners Labyrinth* recommended sowing 'parsnep' in well manured ground in high summer for eating in Lent the following year. Used to make wine and to sweeten cakes in the days when honey was the only other major source of sugar, its sweetness and starch content has ensured it has been grown in the kitchen garden ever since.

Curiously, when the parsnip reached Virginia in 1609 it was held in high esteem by the native Americans, but largely ignored by the north Americans. Perhaps this was because the native Americans in the southwest and Mexico were accustomed to making a meal out of the baked, ground root of the wild parsnip. In Britain meanwhile, and so long as north European Protestants still regarded the potato as only fit for 'pigs and papists' the parsnip was the preferred accompaniment to roast beef.

Another seasonal accompaniment were **broad beans**, *Vicia faba*, which like the faba, field, winter, tick or horse bean had been cultivated since biblical times. Ancient broad bean-like seeds 8,500 years old have been found in the Middle East and the seeds probably reached northern Europe in the hand luggage of the Roman centurion. Originally a black coloured bean, the broad bean was a valuable crop which could be eaten fresh or stored dry until needed, and the plant's nitrogen-fixing qualities endeared it to the gardener. It was such a prize crop that, by the Middle Ages, the crime of stealing beans from open fields carried the death penalty. The bean had its own revenge for it had a fierce reputation for flatulence: 'Broad beans are very nutritious, but are not easily digested and should not be given to invalids,' warned the cautious author of one kitchen encyclopaedia. The poet William Butler Yeats was untroubled by its notoriety; he wrote in *The Lake Isle of Innisfree*, published in 1893:

> I will arise and go now, and go to Innisfree,
> And a small cabin build there, of clay and wattles made;
> Nine beans rows will I have there, a hive for the honey bee,
> And live alone in the bee-loud glade

Exercising poetic licence, Yeats did not mention whether he preferred the broad bean or one of the many garden beans that had originated on the other side of the world – America.

OUT OF AMERICA

European gardeners owe a debt of gratitude to the American Indians for their protein rich maize, squash, potatoes and **beans**. The new American civilisation owes its very existence to them.

Forty years before Yeats penned his poem, that contemplative gardener Henry David Thoreau was planning his own Indian bean patch, on the shores of Walden Pond at Concord, Massachusetts. 'What shall I learn of beans or beans of me? I cherish them, I hoe them, early and late I have an eye to them and this is my days work.'

Thoreau, however, did not eat his beans but sold them to buy rice. He was growing 'the common small white bush bean', one of more than fifty varieties of *Phaseolus*, all originating from the Americas and embracing French, navy, flageolet, snap, *haricot vert*, scarlet or runner bean (*Phaseolus coccineus*), and the Lima or butter bean (*Phaseolus lunatus*).

A Webbs Seed catalogue for 1888 noted: 'The Kidney Bean, *Phaseolus vulgaris,* has been cultivated for a considerable time, but there is uncertainty as to whether it was known in Europe before the discovery of America, where the genus is strongly represented.' It was not: the kidney bean, which still grows wild in South America, came into Europe in the sixteenth century stashed alongside the Spanish *conquistadores'* captured gold. When the scarlet-flowered runner bean reached the royal gardens of England during the reign of Charles I it was grown purely for its pretty flowers. It was not until the early 1700s that Chelsea Physic Garden's Philip Miller advocated cooking and eating the green pods.

Spanish *conquistadores* also brought the **capsicum pepper**, *Capsicum fructescens* to their mother country in the 1500s. They called it the *pimento* and the Italians took the *pepperone* to heart, making it an indispensable ingredient in their kitchen recipes. The capsicum, when dried and crushed, was popular elsewhere in Europe because it served as an acceptable substitute for pepper at a time when true black peppercorns were proving too expensive for the kitchen table.

When the Italian explorer Christopher Columbus (1451–1506) brought back yet another 'new' Latin American crop, **maize**, the old Mexican name, *cintli*, was substituted for the Spanish *maiz* instead. (Columbus had discovered the crop growing in Cuba where it was known by the local people as *maisi*). *Zea mays,* a member of the grass family, was to become one of the world's most popular crops. Variously known as corn, sweet corn, Indian corn, mealies, corn-on-the cob and popcorn, it was originally cultivated by Native Americans and not only sustained the Toltecs, Aztecs, Mayas and Incas, but also the 'new' American civilisation: in 1810 the population of America was around 7 million, including nearly 2 million slaves. Largely fed on maize, it had risen to 92 million a century later.

Within a century of being brought to Spain, maize had spread across the globe. The bombastic British farmer-journalist William Cobbett (1712–1786) spoke of it growing in Britain by 1803 ('the very best [for] hog-fattening') and although it was, and still is, fed to cows, it became, in the form of cornflakes or corn on the cob, a favourite British food. Maize was venerated for its legendary figures. There was the Mexican goddess of plenty, Cinteotl, and the American Indian Mondamin, a green giant who was killed and buried by Hiawatha. The maize plant that rose up from Mondamin's grave saved Hiawatha's people from a winter's starvation.

Since the sugar in the corn starts to convert to starch the moment it is picked, sweet corn is best when picked and eaten fresh from the kitchen garden: 'the principle of the lathe is adopted in eating them,' explained the English gardener Edward Bunyard (1878–1939) helpfully in the 1930s. Bunyard was also an enthusiastic supporter of another American import, the marrow: 'We may use it for jam, pies, soup, etc., its merit being its placid acceptance of all flavours.'

Marrows, **pumpkins** and **squashes** are all members of cucurbita genus which originated in the Americas and had arrived in Europe within fifty years of Columbus' voyages. Seeds have been found on ancient Mexican sites and the cucurbits formed a staple part of the diet, along with maize and beans, of Native American Indians (Columbus conferred the description 'Indios' on all the natives he encountered) along America's east coast. When the first Pilgrim Fathers landed at Cape Cod, Massachusetts in 1620 those who survived starvation were rescued by Patuxet tribespeople who taught them how to grow pumpkins among their corn, burying a herring beneath the crop as fertiliser. In October 1621 the settlers ate a ceremonial meal of boiled pumpkins as a thanksgiving for their survival. Although the recipe has been improved, the custom has continued.

The name squash came from the Algonquin Indians and the pumpkin from the Greek, and later Old French, *poumpon*. In terms of alternative uses, the cucurbita are the world's most versatile vegetable: in their different forms, they have served as cups, bottles, the back-scrubbing loofah, soaps, household ornaments, yak fodder and even the legendary birthplace of the Burmese people.

While we are used to a pale- or yellow-fleshed **potato**, *Solanum tuberosum,* those growing still in the wilds of South America, from where they originated, range in colour from yellow and red through to purple and black. The horticultural Incas built terraces and aqueducts to feed their potatoes, which were cultivated as a storage crop and which complemented the maize, grown at lower levels. (Growing potatoes for seed in a cold, blight-free climate benefited the tubers and explains why Scotland traditionally produced the best seed potatoes in Britain.)

In 1537 a party of Spanish soldiers led by Gonzalo Jiménez de Quesada was looting native homes in Sorocotá, a village in present-day Colombia, when they stumbled on a larder of maize, beans and truffle-like tubers. Grown in the tropical forests of the northern Andes, these earthy truffles, '*turmas de tierra*' were almost certainly carried back to Spain and up the river Guadalquivir to Seville. There is some confusion here as the sweet potato, *Ipomaea batatas,* which had been discovered in Haiti by the explorer Columbus, was also being imported to southern Spain around this time. The potato travelled on to Italy as *tartuf-flo*, and into France as *cantoufle* or *truffe,* but it arrived in England in the 1590s by a different route and with a different name.

John Gerard mentions the 'potatoe of Virginia in 1597'. Gerard, a London barber-surgeon, was an enthusiastic gardener who not only managed several of London's society gardens, but also looked after his own plot of ground in Holborn. Here he grew 'all the rare simples' and 'strange trees, herbes, rootes, plants, flowers, and other such rare things.' When in 1596 he catalogued his plants, the year before his famous *Herbal* was published, the potato appeared in the inventory. When the second issue of the *Herbal* was published, Gerard dedicated it to Sir Walter Raleigh, who, some say, introduced the first pinch of tobacco and the first potato to Britain.

'To England the potatoe found its way ... being brought from Virginia by the colonists sent out by Sir Walter Raleigh in 1584, and who returned in July 1586, and "probably," according to Sir Joseph Banks, " brought with them the potatoe",' explained John Claudius Loudon in 1824.

The story goes that Raleigh came by both potato and tobacco through another English knight, Sir Francis Drake. Drake, who had been battling with the Spaniards in the Caribbean, sailed for England after collecting some provisions including potatoes at Cartagena, Colombia. Drake also picked up a group of Virginian colonists who had had enough of the hard life and wanted to return home. Drake's ship, The Golden Hind, berthed in Cork in southern Ireland, leaving a few of his potatoes with Raleigh who grew them on at his Youghal home in County Cork. Raleigh's gardener is said to have sent the poisonous potato fruit to the kitchen rather than the root. The rest arrived in Britain, possibly in Lancashire, but Gerard, confusing the returning colonists with the vegetable, cultivated them under the name *Battata Virginiana,* the Virginian potato.

The **tomato,** *Lycopersicum esculentum,* like the potato, came from South America. The ancient ancestors of the fat, red tomato grew wild on the riverbanks of Peru and Ecuador, and grows there still. When it spread into Central America and Mexico resourceful American Indians brought it into cultivation. Spanish *conquistadores* came across what the Indians called *tomatl* and shipped the fruit back to Seville from where it travelled to Italy. In 1544 one Italian writer recommended cooking the tomato 'like an eggplant – fried in oil with salt and pepper.' He called the fruit *'mala aurea'* or golden apple. Linnaeus classified it as *L. esculentum,* but its supposed links with mandrake (*Mandragon autumnalis*), a notorious narcotic which reportedly shrieked when pulled from the ground, branded the tomato a dangerous fruit, good only for table decoration. 'In Spaine and those hot regions they used to eat prepared and boil'd with pepper, salt and oil; but they yield very little nourishment to the body and the same naught and corrupt,' claimed Gerard. John Parkinson described it in terms with which those prejudiced against the tomato would agree: it was, he wrote, 'full of slimie juice and waterie pulp'.

In Europe the tomato became what the French called *pomme d'amour* or love apple, a reference to its supposed aphrodisiac qualities. Its powers to promote promiscuity earned it yet another name – mad or rage apple. Although the American president Thomas Jefferson was content to grow them in his Monticello garden in the 1780s, the tomato clearly needed further promotion. In 1820, Robert Gibbon Johnson helped it along by publicly eating a basket of tomatoes on the steps of the courthouse in Salem, New Jersey to dispel the myth that the tomato was poisonous. The argument over whether it was a fruit or a vegetable (and thus earns a place in this book) was settled by an American court of law. John Nix, seeking to avoid a 10% tax on vegetables imported to the US, claimed the tomato was a fruit. The Supreme Court in 1893 ruled that, while the tomato, like the cucumber and squash, was a 'fruit of a vine', these were all 'in the common language of the people ... vegetables which are grown in the kitchen garden.'

OUT IN THE COLD

One vegetable that was almost lost to the kitchen garden is the **skirret** (*Sium sisarum*), a perennial tap-rooted plant which originated in China and was grown in Britain for centuries (as early as 1275 according to ecclesiastical records). In Scotland the skirret was cultivated under the name of crummock while the gentleman gardener John Worlidge described skirrets as 'the sweetest, whitest, and most pleasant of roots' in 1682, around the same time as the Bishop of Carlisle's wife Elizabeth was preparing her marrow, date and skirrits pie: 'Take Skirrits being boyl'd & peel'd, put fome of them into ye pye …'). Shakespeare made mention of them in his *Merry Wives of Windsor* as the Elizabethan poet Michael Drayton (1563–1631) hinted at their capacity to arouse: 'The Skirret (which some say) in sallats, stirs the blood' (*Poly-olbion*, 1623). The vegetable had almost disappeared from the twentieth-century seed catalogues until it was revived by heritage vegetable plant growers.

The **swede**, on the other hand, slipped into the culinary wilderness in the mid 1900s as the result of cheap school dinners and a heavy reliance on the vegetable during World War Two. Jane Grigson, in her *Vegetable Book*, judged 'the watery orange slush … unredeemable by drainage or butter.' In the root bed the swede was a close cousin of the turnip and commonly confused with it in the vegetable taxonomy. When the swede was taken to America it arrived with its Swedish name of ram's root or *rotbagga*. The **turnip**, from the Latin *napus,* became in the 1500s the *neip* in Britain, but when, on Burn's Night, a haggis was put on the hob along with *neips,* the *neips* were swedes and not turnips.

WHAT'S IN A NAME

The curious names given to some vegetables may shed light on their different histories. Was it medieval Crusaders, returning to Europe from their battles in the Holy Land, who brought seeds of the Persian *ispanai* or *isfanai* (our spinach) home? Did the French bean really originate in France? Did the eating of cucumbers cause such offence that someone had to invent a burpless variety? And why do Americans grow zucchini when the British raise courgettes?

The bean provides a starting point for some linguistic origins, and confusions. Take the dwarf kidney bean, also known as the French bean and in France *haricot vert,* a tender bean eaten pod and all, and *haricot jaune,* podded and harvested for the seed. *Haricot* comes from its Aztec name, *ayacotl,* but it became the French bean only because of the Gallic gardeners who cultivated it. The French *flageolet* bean was so called either because it looked like a flute or *flageolet* or was a corruption of *Phaseolus.* (It was the French, too, who gave the 'Hasty' pea, a large and early variety, its name – from *hâtif* or early.)

Phaseolus, the Latin name for a small, fast-sailing craft, referred to the canoe-like shape of the bean pod while the kidney bean itself earned its name from its similarity to that part of the body. The climbing bean was known to gardeners at the court of Charles 1 as the 'runner' bean. It had been collected in Virginia, USA by the King's gardener John Tradescant and given to the monarch as a decorative plant. In its homeland, however, it became a string bean, a reference to the stringy seams that run down each side of the pod.

When the *Phaseolus* began to supplement the old-fashioned field, Celtic and broad bean (all varieties of *Vicia faba*) John Gerard spoke with surprise of being able to eat them 'cods and all.' Favourite varieties in the early 1800s included the Windsor, so-called by Huguenot gardeners simply because Windsor happened to be a profitable place to grow them, and the Mazagan.

'Sow the first crop of early (pea) varieties, rolling the seed in red lead, and filling the drills half full over the peas with chopped furze' (bracken) 'or chopped barley chaff. Sow dwarf Peas in pot. Plant Mazagan Bean, and treat in the same way,' advised the *Illustrated Guide for Amateur Gardeners* of 1876.

Mazagan was a small Portuguese settlement on the coast of Morocco and seed from the settlement promised to produce a well-flavoured, early crop. The English naturalist, Reverend Gilbert White, was already well ahead of the pack when he wrote in his *Garden Kalendar* on 2 November 1754: 'Started ten rows of Mazagan-beans (never planted in England) in the field garden.'

As for the potato, another vegetable championed by the good vicar of Selbourne in Hampshire, it was the Peruvians who referred to it as *papas* and hence its one-time French name, *la papas des Péruviens*. In Wales the potato became *pytatws* and in the Scottish vernacular *tatties,* which sounds more like the Spanish name for the sweet potato, *batatas.*

Another linguistic throwback concerns the 'ridge' cucumber, so called for its habit of climbing over the old-fashioned ridges in the ridge and channel system of vegetable growing. The cucumber, especially in the raw, was viewed with some suspicion by English Victorian gentlemen who preferred to eat it stewed and served in a white sauce. The arrival of a burpless variety calmed all fears of an accidental, tea-time belch and the uncooked cucumber went on to become the staple sandwich filling at vicarage tea parties.

And finally, why do Americans whose 'squash' seeds were taken to Europe in the 1500s now find themselves eating 'zucchini'? It was the Italian immigrants who reintroduced the courgette to its place of origin, along with their name for it.

A Good Idea at the Time: Container Gardening

The popularity of container gardening has grown in proportion to the diminishing size of the average garden. But in Roman times, the men and women who looked after the Roman Emperor Tiberius' gardens turned container gardening into craft. The emperor was mad about cucumbers and expected, as emperors do, to be able to eat them at any, and every, time of the year. Terrified of the emperor's wrath, his gardeners invented a system of growing the cucumbers on portable beds. If cold weather threatened, the beds were wheeled inside to safety. On cool days they were taken out of doors, and sheltered behind windows made of mica, a translucent stone cut into sheets for the purpose.

The Secret of Selling Seeds

The seed is the beginning of all things. '*Germination* is that act of operation of the vegetative principle by which the embryo is extricated from its envelopes, and converted into a plant. This is universally the first part of the process of vegetation. For it may be regarded as an indubitable fact, that all plants spring originally from seed.'

So wrote John Claudius Loudon in his *Encyclopaedia of Gardening*. It was published in 1822 shortly after the seed merchants, Messers Sutton and Son, distributed a printed list of the seeds they sold. It was not the nation's first seed catalogue – seed sellers and nursery people had been advertising their wares in newspapers and magazines for a half a century or more – but it was the first to offer the kitchen gardener a current price list and useful advice on when and how to plant their vegetable seed. It was also the first of many devices designed to ensure that a well-thumbed copy of the seed catalogue survived the growing season and was still on hand in winter when it was time to reorder seeds.

At first seed companies relied on the fine and often inspirational line drawings of their artists and the enthusiastic sincerity of their copywriters to sell their wares. 'With great satisfaction we now introduce a new White Kidney which we have had under trial for several years. It was raised by the late Mr. Clark, the raiser of our Magnum Bonum, Abundance, and other heavy cropping varieties, and combines the high quality of Victoria in its best days with the productiveness of White Elephant. The yield has astonished experienced growers to whom we sent small parcels for trial.'

The subject of this entry in a Sutton's seed catalogue was the potato, Sutton Perfection. Sutton's and other catalogue editors were quick to learn the value of publishing testimonials alongside advertisements for 'The Student Parsnep', the 'Red-top Mousetail Turnip' and the 'Prince of Wales, a heavy cropping Pea, which has long been popular with amateurs and cottagers.'

'I have cut Cucumbers from your Berks Champion three weeks earlier than any of my neighbours,' boasted the Reverend J.R. Barlow of Pertenhall, Kimbolton with a singular lack of modesty in a Sutton catalogue for 1881.

The people who paid the seed bills were the gentry, even if it was their head gardeners who ordered them, and the catalogues could be both obsequious − 'Gentlemen are respectfully invited to have price from us before ordering elsewhere' − and charitable: 'From your beautiful and valuable Amateur's Guide, I have made a common labouring lad into a most excellent practical Gardener,' wrote Mrs Parsons from The Castle, Buttevant, County Cork. 'I do not see anywhere nicer work or so good things as he grows, and all his education has been from one of your Guides.'

Colour printing processes transformed the appearance − but not the prose − of the seed catalogues in the second half of the 1800s just as the American seed market, previously a profitable source of income for European seed growers, developed its own seed industry. In their battles for supremacy, the 800 or so US seed merchants proved to be innovative marketeers. There were free gifts of seeds and more testimonials: 'The package of Vandergaw Cabbage you sent me did much better than the Large Late Flat Dutch.' There were promotions, price wars and prizes: 'We offer, for 1888, CASH PRIZES OF $25.00 and $10.00 for the two largest onions raised from seed purchased of us this year – the onions, or reliable affidavits of their weights, to be sent to us before Nov. 1st,' promised the authors of the Burpee catalogue, which in 1888 ran to 128 pages, most of them devoted to vegetables.

Then there were slick slogans. 'Seeds That Yield are Sold by Field' was the catch phrase of Henry Field who had started out on horseback selling seed around Shenandoah in the 1890s. By the 1920s he was running his own country music radio station and selling his seeds on air.

In France meanwhile, one of the nation's most senior seed firms, Vilmorin, devised a clever strategy for selling their products: the picture. The company was based on an old family firm, Le Febvre, run by Pierre Geoffroy. In 1782 Geoffroy's daughter Claude, or Mâitresse Grainière (the Seed Mistress) as she was known, and her husband Pierre Andrieux, botanist to Louis XIV, opened a shop on the Mégisserie Quay in Paris. The business, later run by their daughter and her husband, Philippe-Victoire De Vilmorin, became Vilmorin-Andrieux and later, Vilmorin Co. Responsible for introducing the field beetroot and 'rutabaga' or swede to France, Philippe-Victoire was also a good publicist. He not only commissioned watercolours to illustrate their catalogues and seed packets, but also ordered a collection of artificial vegetables to be exhibited at the Paris Universal Exhibition in 1855. Made of plaster, each was a perfect replica in weight and colour of the vegetable itself.

Seed salespeople learned to be economical with the truth, picturing on their seed packets and catalogues magnificently exaggerated versions of their produce. The underlying aim was, as it has become and ever more will be, to appeal to the aspirational gardener.

It was not always so. Plain vegetable seed was being sold, without any trimmings, from The Strand in London in the late 1600s. The garden historian John Harvey has traced at least five nurseries in and around the capital at that time, the largest, London and Wise, occupying 100 acres of what would later become the site of the Albert Hall and the South Kensington Museum.

The sale of vegetable seed, measured by the bushel and hundredweight, was a lucrative business worth over half a million pounds a year. While it was concentrated on the south-east, each region contributed its own regional specialities to what Loudon called the 'Middlesex seed market held twice a week in a large roofed space in Mark-lane. The purchasers are the London retailers, or the wholesale dealers for their country customers.' Kent gardeners brought their radish, kidney beans, turnips, 'toker or Sandwich beans' and onions; Berkshire men brought their cabbages and white skinned or Reading onion seeds while in Worcestershire and Warwickshire the market gardeners took their seeds of white onions, asparagus, cucumber and carrot to the Birmingham markets. In Leicestershire, Loudon noted, 'the farmers, tho often rich, have seldom good gardens.'

Seed was also sold by stall holders, costermongers and barrow boys at country markets across the land. Those who chose not to buy, or could not afford to do so, carefully collected and stored their own seed in mouse-proof draws and rat-proof safes, despite the advice of garden writers such as Shirley Hibberd: 'the professional seed-grower will beat you nine times out of ten ... and if you deal with none but respectable seedsmen, and avoid the cheap rubbish that is vended in odd corners, you will save a good deal of labour.'

Thomas Tusser, however, had been in favour of trading seed locally: 'One seed for another to make an exchange/With fellowly neighbours seemeth not strange,' he suggested in 1580. Home seed was selected, not from some stunted individual, which had been missed during the harvest, but from the earliest, healthiest and most vigorous vegetables. Carrots and cabbages, which formed seed in their second year, were lifted whole in their first autumn. The carrots, after their foliage was cut back, were buried or clamped in beds of peat or sand. The brassicas, their root balls still intact, were tenderly wrapped in cloth and hung from the rafters of a dry shed where they held their breath until spring when they could be replanted and their seed harvested when it was set. Alternatively, the cabbage could be buried outside. 'Market gardeners and many private individuals, raise seed for their own use,' wrote Loudon. 'Some of the handsomest cabbages ... are dug up in autumn, and sunk in the ground to the head; early next summer a flower-stem appears, which is followed by an abundance of seed. It is mentioned in Bastien, that the seed-growers of Aubervilliers have learned by experience, that seed gathered from the middle flower-stem produces plants which will be fit for use a fortnight earlier.'

Well ripened and dried, the seed would keep for six to eight years, he added, confirming the conviction that seed improved with age. For example, three to four years was judged ideal for cucumber seed while soaking the seed in sheep's milk or mead (the alcoholic drink made from fermented honey) prevented the fruit from turning bitter.

Success was guaranteed if seed was 'sown dry and set wet' and poor soil was usually blamed for the failure of seed to set true or perform like its parent. Once Carl Linnaeus revealed that cross pollination between different varieties of the same species was the problem, seedspeople began to exploit this characteristic to improve, or enoble, vegetable seeds. Webbs' Seeds announced the arrival of their new, cross-breed pea, the Wordsley Wonder in 1888:

This wonderful Pea is the result of crosses between Advancer, Little Gem, and Prizetaker, and whilst possessing all the good qualities of the two former varieties, it has both the constitution and productiveness of the latter. As a first early Pea for large gardens, it is unequalled, and its convenient height and cropping properties render it indispensable to the amateur.

So the practice of improving seed, although not necessarily for the good of the gardener continued until, in the 1960s, the F1 hybrids which had been developed in the 1920s began to emerge. The F of F1 stood for *filia,* Latin for daughter, and the seeds promised to revolutionise the kitchen garden, developed as they were by crossing two selected lines to produce vigorous growth from dependable seed. But, like the genetically modified seed that would follow in its wake, it had one great advantage to the seed merchant and one disadvantage to the gardener: it did not set true seed. The gardener was obliged to return to their seed catalogue year after year.

And it is the gardener's little winter bible, the seed catalogue, that reveals how times have changed in the seed industry. One of France's oldest nursery firms, Vilmorin-Andrieux, which published a 100-page catalogue in 1771, produced a list of vegetables suitable for 'cold and temperate climates' in 1885. The list offered 58 beets, 145 cabbages, 74 onions and no less than 170 different peas. A century later in 2003 a British seed catalogue could offer only 6 beetroot, 20 cabbages, 5 onions and 10 varieties of peas.

CARL LINNAEUS AND THE CLASSIFICATION OF VEGETABLES

Jan: 20. Hot-bed works very well. Hard frost for two or three days: now ground covered with snow. One of the hyacinths in the glafses seems to promise to blow soon.

22. On this day, which was very bright, the sun shone very warm on the Hot-bed from a quarter before nine to three quarters after two. Very hard frost.

29. On this day the mercury in the weather-glafses, which
had been mounting leisurely for many days, was got one full
degree above settled fair in the parlour, & within half a degree
of the same in the study.

The Reverend Gilbert White's *Garden Kalendar* for 1758 reflects
the winter preoccupation of every vegetable gardener: the cold.
In 1758 gardeners across the northern world watched the mercury fall at night and rise by day. Then, as now, they measured
the temperature against the Celsius scale devised by Anders
Celsius. For reasons best known to himself, however, Anders
calibrated his scale so that nought represented the boiling point
of water and 100 degrees its freezing point. Today we would be
complaining still of a mild frost of 103 degrees had it not been
for a chance meeting between Anders' uncle, the genial Olaf
Rudbeck, and an impoverished Swedish student, Carl Linnaeus,
at Uppsala in 1729. Rudbeck took the 22-year-old in and fed
him. Linnaeus would later persuade Olaf's nephew Anders to
reverse his calibration.

Linnaeus not only set the standard calibration for the kitchen
garden thermometer, he also learned how to grow bananas successfully in the Netherlands and set the standards for modern
botanical gardens such as National Botanical Garden of Wales
and the Eden Project in Cornwall. But his most important
contribution to the vegetable world was to devise a system of
classifying vegetables and every other living form. While one
colleague described his work as 'lewd and licentious', Linnaeus
had the satisfaction of having his system of classification adopted
around the globe. We use it still today.

Carl Linnaeus was born in a simple turf-roofed timber cabin
at Råshult near the shores of Lake Mökeln in the southern
province of Sweden on 23 May 1707, the oldest child of Nils
Ingemarsson Linnaeus. Nils had adopted the name Linnaeus
when he attended the university at Uppsala, taking the title
from a favourite tree that had grown at a former family home.

The tree was a lime or linden; forty years later it would become *Tilia cordata,* thanks to Linnaeus.

Nils was the parish priest and a fanciful gardener. He once created a curious raised bed to represent the family dining table with shrubs to portray the dinner guests sitting down to a meal. Carl was as intrigued by this horticultural oddity as he was by the natural world in general. Even at five, out walking with his father, Nils would quiz Carl on the local names of plants. Nils is said to have reprimanded the boy and told him to commit the correct names to memory.

He also gave the child a plot of his own to cultivate. The garden is a good educator and Carl, like his younger brother Samuel, became a committed naturalist and gardener. This passion for gardening had unfortunate consequences for Samuel Linnaeus. Some years later when Carl failed to follow in his father's footsteps and become a priest, his tutor told his parents that the young man's academic shortcomings were entirely due to his horticultural obsession. Fearing that Samuel would prove a second disappointment, Linnaeus' mother banned Samuel from meddling with plants. (The boy turned his attention to bees instead, a subject on which he would become a world authority.)

Carl went to study medicine rather than theology at his father's old university in Uppsala. Here he became friends with Peter Artedi, a fellow student who shared his fascination for the natural world. The two young men hatched an ambitious plan: together they would classify all of God's plants and creatures in a systematic fashion.

Until then every vegetable and plant had a variety of local or vernacular names and several, sometimes conflicting, Latin names. A Greek physician, Dioscorides, had diligently named some 500 plants in his *De Materia Medica* around the time of Christ, but it took almost a thousand years before his work was disseminated first through the Arabic and then the Latin world.

Linnaeus and Artedi divided the task of classifying the animal and plant kingdoms between them and swore that whoever finished first would then come to the aid of his friend. But in 1735 Artedi drowned when he fell into an Amsterdam canal. Linnaeus took on all the work himself. By the time he died in 1778, (some say of overwork) Linnaeus had introduced a system for naming vegetables – and every other plant – that endures to this day.

Botanists and naturalists were agreed that plants fell into families. Onions, leeks, and garlic, for example, belonged to the allium family; beans and peas to the legume family; cabbages and cauliflowers to the brassica family; sweet corn to the grass family. What Linnaeus did was to introduce a two-word name for every plant within the families.

Plant families could be subdivided into distinct groups (or genera) and Linnaeus used the genus for the first name: *Pastinaca* from the Latin *pascare* (to feed) for the parsnip, for example, and *Pisum* for the pea. Each group or genus could be divided again, this time into species. Linnaeus used his second Latin name to denote the species so the garden pea became *Pisum sativa* as distinct from the Mediterranean pea, *Pisum elatium*. Finally, each species could be further divided to include cultivated varieties or cultivars. As well as inventing a standard use of Latin words for every plant, Linnaeus also provided an international starting point for the old botanical names when he published his *Species Plantarum* in 1753.

Linnaeus classified the genus and species of plants according to the number of stamens and stigmas, a 'sexual system' of classification. One of his friends was John Siegesbeck, a St Petersburg academic after whom Linnaeus named the Sigesbeckia. But the two fell out when Siegesbeck denounced his former friend's work as 'lewd'. How, he ranted, could onions be up to such vegetative immorality? What was worse: how could young people be taught 'so licentious a method' of classification? Yet, despite the 'loathsome harlotry' of his system, it was adopted universally and Linnaeus became a household name.

Linnaeus also showed the kitchen gardener that the successful cultivation of any vegetable depended on duplicating as closely as possible the plant's natural origins, soil and climate. (He would later advise the curators of botanical gardens to keep separate hot, warm and cold glasshouses as well as an outdoor area so that they might replicate local growing conditions, which laid the foundations for contemporary dome gardens such as the Eden project.)

In spite of his celebrity status, Linnaeus was a modest man. For his funeral arrangements he stipulated: 'Entertain nobody at my funeral, and accept no condolences.' But when he died on 22 January 1778, his instructions were ignored. A stately funeral was held at Uppsala Cathedral and even the King of Sweden came to pay his respects to the man who gave a name to every vegetable in the world.

JOHN LOUDON'S CULTIVATION ADVICE FOR 'PRACTICAL MEN'

When John Claudius Loudon arrived in London at the age of twenty in 1803, he reached the capital during a period of social change that would transform his fortunes – and the contents of the kitchen garden. The economics of industrial revolution produced abject poverty and unimagined wealth. Loudon would help those with the money to spend it on their gardens: 'Every man who does not limit the vegetable parts of his dinner to bread and potatoes, is a patron of gardening, by creating a demand for its productions,' he would write later. 'He is a consumer, which is the first species of patron, and the more valuable varieties are such as regularly produce a dessert after dinner, and maintain throughout the year beautiful nosegays and pots of flowers in their lobbies and drawing rooms.'

The gritty Scot had moved to London meaning to set himself up as a landscape gardener. He arrived with a letter of recommendation from one of his botanic professors at Edinburgh University addressed to Sir Joseph Banks. Thirty-five years earlier Banks had sailed with Captain Cook on the Endeavour, seen Botany Bay so named, and brought back a raft of new plants. A former scientific adviser to King George, Banks possessed a botanical knowledge to match the vast library in his Soho Square home and was now running the botanical gardens at Kew. He provided the perfect introduction for the young, ambitious Mr Loudon.

Within a year of meeting Banks, Loudon had written his first book and over the next forty years, as literacy grew and print costs fell, Loudon turned out horticultural works that appealed to the new, middle-class market. When his books became nineteenth century best sellers, he founded his *Gardener's Magazine*, one of the early popular gardening periodicals in which he promised to 'record, as they occur, the various discoveries, acquisitions, and improvements that are constantly making in gardening ... and to render them available to practical men.' Furthermore, wrote the shrewd journalist, his magazine's advertising section would prove just the place to discover where to procure 'paints, cements, manures, [and] compositions for destroying insects, such as Davidson's destroyer of earth worms.'

When in 1811 the sale of the lease on his Oxfordshire farm put £15,000 into Loudon's pocket, he set off across Europe to find out how foreigners managed their vegetable plots. He found little to admire: 'The culinary vegetables of France have not been increased from the earliest period of horticultural history, with the exception of the sea-cale and the potatoe. In salading and legumes they far excel most countries; but in the cabbage tribe, turnips, and potatoes, they are inferior to the moister climates of Holland and Britain.'

Of Russia he wrote:

The potatoe is but lately introduced, and that only in a few places. Many of the peasants refuse to eat or cultivate this root, from mere prejudice, and from an idea very natural to a people in a state of slavery, that any thing proposed by their lords must be for the lord's advantage, and not theirs; thus the first handful of food thrown to untamed animals operates as a scare.

In Italy, things were little better:

Italian cucumbers are never so succulent as those grown in our humid frames by dung-heat. The love-apple, egg-plant, and capsicum, are extensively cultivated near Rome and Naples for the kitchen; the fruit of the first attaining a larger size, and exhibiting the most grotesque forms. Of culinary vegetables the Italians began with those left them by the Romans, and they added the potatoe to their number as soon as, or before, we did. Though the Italians have the advantage over the rest of Europe in fruits, that good is greatly counterbalanced by the inferiority of their culinary vegetables.

Loudon never travelled to America, but he gleaned enough details from publications such as seeds man B. McMahon's *American Kalendar* to observe: 'Culinary vegetables grow in the same perfection as in England, excepting the cauliflower and some species of beans. Water-melons, musk-melons, squashes, sweet potatoes, cucumbers, &c. arrive at great perfection.' The growing of squash was of particular interest: 'The seeds of pumpkin are scattered in the field, when planting the corn, and no further trouble is necessary than throwing them into the wagon when ripe.'

John Claudius Loudon died in December 1843, his death marking the end of an era, but one in which the cause of the common vegetable had been well advanced.

Vegetable cornucopia: a trug filled with treasures from the kitchen garden, including carrots, cabbages, cauliflowers and chillies.

Well contained: an abandoned air-raid shelter is pressed into service to contain the compost heap.

Walled in: a kitchen garden wall in herringbone-style pattern protects the crops.

Two feet apart: the principal unit of measurement in the kitchen garden was the human body.

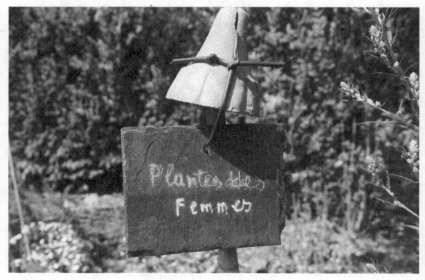

Plantes des femmes: slate and chalk serve a useful function in a *jardin potager*.

Wildly successful: many gardeners have adopted an organic approach in the kitchen garden to encourage insects and other wildlife.

Pest control: a home-made scarecrow designed to frighten the birds away from a plot holder's patch.

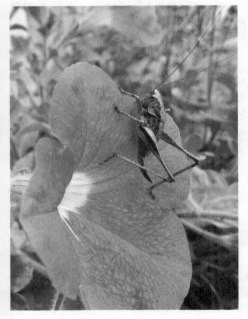

Damage limitation: holding off with the herbicides and pesticides has a beneficial effect on insects.

Ancient peas: archaeological seed remains suggest the pea is one of our oldest vegetables.

Southern promise: the vegetables that came out of the Americas would transform the kitchen gardens of Europe.

Huertas verduras: the Moorish people left behind a rich horticultural heritage when they departed from Spain.

Mysterious properties: the globe artichoke, along with the tomato and the potato, was regarded as an aphrodisiac.

Cabbages and compost: a group of like-minded people met in Ramsgate, Kent, to form the first Vegetarian Society in 1847.

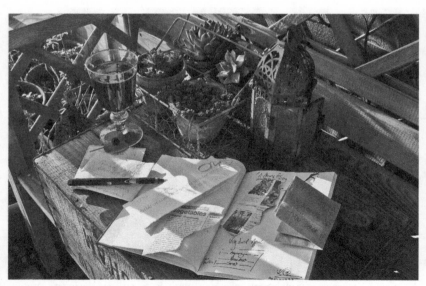

Seeding ideas: the gardener's diary records the season's successes and failures.

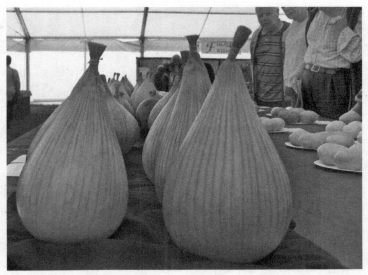

Giant attraction: mammoth onions draw a crowd on the National Vegetable Society's stand at Malvern Royal Horticultural Society Show.

Political potatoes: 'not a mere vegetable, but rather . . . an instrument of destiny.'

Pesticide free? British government scientists concluded in 2016 that pesticide residues on many vegetables, although 'above reporting levels', would not have an effect on health.

War effort: two First World War Land Army women hoe brassicas in a Herefordshire orchard.

Family fun: the freshest vegetables are those that are sown, grown and harvested from the allotment.

4

Vegetable Bounty

A VEGETABLE HERBAL

Superfoods such as sweet potato and avocado, leafy greens and beans, garlic and ginger come with the promise of perfect health and disease prevention. Or so we are told. However, there is nothing new in the idea of a healthy diet. If the biblical Garden of Eden, with its temptingly forbidden fruit, was a place of paradise, the down-to-earth kitchen garden was a place of healing. John Gerard, for example, advised that lettuce 'cooleth the heat of the stomacke, called the heart-burning; and helpeth it when it is troubled with choler; it quencheth thirst, and causeth sleepe.' The fruit of the cucumber, meanwhile, 'cut in pieces or chopped as herbes to the pot' and taken three times a day 'doth perfectly cure all manner of sauce flegme and copper faces, red and shining fieries noses ... and such like precious faces'.

Much of the information about the vegetable herbal reached Europe from Africa and the Middle East. Following their invasion of Persia in the seventh century, Arab conquerors retained and conserved the civilised Persian gardens, which were stocked with useful plants. (They also acquired the Persian word 'paradise', literally a walled garden.) The conquering Moors carried this horticultural knowledge and their pharmaceutical texts with them as they moved up through Spain in the 800s bringing with them their citrus fruits and 'new' vegetables such as cauliflowers, red-rooted carrots, cardoons, aubergines and artichokes. Artichokes were celebrated for their aphrodisiac properties, although the aubergine was regarded with suspicion: while the Moors could consume them with impunity, it was said that Christians risked death if they ate them.

This sometimes suspect knowledge was carried up into Europe, especially through the royal courts: kings and queens naturally expected to benefit from the very latest medicinal advice. Scholars, too, carried the plant pharmacology from monastery to monastery: while God was seen as the chief physician in the medieval hierarchy, monks and nuns were expected to do what they could to alleviate suffering. The sick and the ill attended the infirmary (the term was carried to the New World by the founding fathers, having outlived its use in Europe) which was served by the infirmarer who, aided by their physic garden, acted as both pharmacist and physician. The physic harboured an arsenal of useful salads, herbs, vegetables and flowers – until the mid 1700s little distinction was made between them. The state of stress, for example, might be treated by bleeding (six times a year), to be followed with nourishing vegetable soups and the quiet stimulation of conversation in the parlour (from *parler* to talk). On the subject of natural bleeding, the twelfth-century German abbess Hildegard von Bingen recommended, for period pains, an ointment made of 'a rose, and half as much sage': 'the place where a person is troubled by cramp or paralysis should be rubbed with it.' However, a male horror of menstruation led to some bizarre ideas such as that a woman 'in her terms' should remain outside the melonry for fear that the fruit would fall. Early 'authorities' declared that if a young woman, menstruating for the first time, was led around the cabbage patch it would kill any caterpillars on the crop, but the gardener had to take care: young plants might expire if a woman in menstruation so much as looked at them.

From the Middle Ages to the late 1800s physicians took a holistic approach to their patients' ills, advocating good air, exercise, rest and, on the premise that a little of what you fancy does you good, a modicum of strong emotions such as pleasure or anxiety. A mother, meanwhile, relied on her hand-me-down down knowledge and experience to care for a sick child or relative. She would be familiar with hedgerow cures, treating worms with vermicidal plants such as mugwort or wormwood, for example, or prescribing salads, pottages and tisanes (an infusion of dried herbs) for a particular condition. Until the 1400s, however, she could only update that knowledge from hearsay since her gender kept her in a state of illiteracy, particularly of the *lingua medicina*, the language of medicine, Latin. Gradually these Latin texts were translated and pirated copies were circulated around the country homes.

So it was she learned that the wild parsnip in a decoction helped the bowels to move and the urine to flow, while oil extracted from the seeds could soothe intermittent fevers such as malaria. From Thomas Hill's *Gardeners Labyrinth* 1577 she discovered even greater benefits: 'Parsnep removeth the venereal act, procureth Urine, and asswageth the Cholerick, sendeth down the Termes in Women; it profiteth the Melanchollicke, encreaseth good blood, helpeth the straightnese of making water, amendeth stitches of the sides or purisies, the bite of venemous beast, it amendeth the eating of Ulcers, the wearing of this root is profitable.' You might feel foolish wearing your *parsnep* but at least you knew it was doing you good.

The leek featured as a cure for an inflammation of the arm when used as a hot poultice. If the housewife could plan ahead, she might take advantage of the knowledge that celery boiled with oil and sweet beer and swallowed four days in a row acted as a contraceptive. Celery would also treat blood-shot eyes if mixed with resinous frankincense and, mixed with any oil, was a salve for sore joints. Wild celery was a laxative and diuretic, relieving swellings and breaking up gallstones. For the prevention of kidney stones, seakale was the answer according to the Hampshire apothecary and noted botanist William Curtis (1746–1799). The up-and-coming potato had its uses too. Early potatoes fetched a high price as an aphrodisiac while a potato was a sure charm against rheumatism – but only if it had been stolen. A slice of potato rubbed over a wart and then buried, caused the wart to disappear. Garlic was recognised for its antiseptic properties, even being pressed into service during World War One, while the onion had a prophetic function: the thickening of onion skins were sure signs of a bad winter approaching. Leaf vegetables were always useful. (Parsley, as we have seen from Peter Rabbit's native knowledge, was a cure for stomach ache. Less well known, except to the Romans, was the idea that parsley could cure sick fish if scattered on the surface of the pond.) Since lettuce, the sacred plant of the Egyptian goddess of fertility, was used in sacrifices, it was forbidden food for the temple priests. For the laity, however, it made a healing poultice and, as Gerard suggested, could cure stomach aches and coughs. While Greeks and Romans ate their lettuces last thing at night to calm the mind and induce sleep, the lettuce also promised to cleanse the blood, promote milk in nursing mothers, counter impotence and cure excessive drinking. (The Romans also thought that eating raw, pickled cabbage before a meal countered the effects of alcohol.)

The bean was another life saver. The American naturalist and essayist Henry Thoreau (1817–1862) noted a Roman passion for beans 'not that I wanted beans to eat, for I am by nature a Pythagorean [meaning he preferred a meat, fish and bean-free diet] so far as beans are concerned, whether they mean porridge or voting,' he declared in 1845. (The Greek Pythagoreans, believing that the soul passed on into another body after death, had an aversion to the foetal-shaped beans which seemed to presage the germ of life, while it was a custom of Roman politicians to distributed free beans during elections to bolster their chances at the polls.) The Celts supposedly celebrated with a beanfeast, Scottish witches reputedly rode not broomsticks, but bean-stalks, and it was expedient to carry a bean or two with you on dark nights: ghosts were sent packing if you spat a bean at them. Gerard noted that the pea was 'not so windy as be the beans', but there were fraudulent overtones to giving a man 'a pea for a bean'. Religious customs had plenty of uses for the vegetable crop. Onions, leeks and colewort were dutifully eaten during Lent while dried carlin, black, or parched (simmered) peas, grown in the north-east of England, were soaked overnight and eaten on Passion or Carlin Sunday. Whether this was a religious rite or a stopgap meal at a time of year when the vegetable plot was depleted is not recorded.

Although Pliny the Elder had recorded no less than eighty-seven cabbage-related medicines, the general view of vegetables through the 1700s and 1800s was that, while they might cure you of one or two ailments, they were often not to be trusted. In the Elizabethan age, for example, the potentially healthy benefits of vegetables were lost on the sailing fraternity who rarely listed fresh vegetables among their ships' provisions. On board, a diet of dried beans was bad enough without adding beetroot, said to cause flatulence, while dysentery and malaria were thought to be symptoms, not of contaminated water or mosquitoes, but the wholly innocent cucumber. Nicholas Culpeper, meanwhile, had already condemned that other salad crop, the radish, in his *Compleat Herbal* of 1642: 'Garden radishes are in wantonness by the gentry eaten as a salad, but they breed but scurvy humours in the stomach, and corrupt the blood, and then send for a physician as fast as you can.'

Not until the 1800s did the Admiralty accept the necessity of dosing its sailors with lemon juice to counter scurvy. In the interests of economy, however, they carried the cheaper, and less effective, limes from the British colonies; ever after the British sailor was referred to as a limey by the Americans. But by the mid 1800s attitudes to vegetables were changing on both sides of the Atlantic. 'The garden pays full as well as the field,' advised a North American farmer in one 1859 periodical. Twenty years later, a Mr Hood was corresponding with the *Canadian Horticulturalist* on the healthy benefits of eating tomatoes, to increase 'one's hopes of longevity. How glorious a thing to be able, like Macbeth, to say "Throw physic to the dogs", and rejoice in the diminution of your doctor's bills.'

In Europe during this period the householder was more concerned by taste than the supposedly healthy benefits of the vegetable although it was soon apparent that those forced to live in the city slums were dying from their impoverished diets. In 1899 when Britain decided it needed healthy recruits to fight the Boers in southern Africa, they found the average farmhand fit enough. Yet 90% of one contingent of over 1,000 volunteers from the city of Manchester were rejected on the grounds of ill health. It took two world wars to drive home the message that greens were good for you. ('Gardens are still in the news,' wrote Toronto columnist Collier Stevenson in 1943 ,'for ... the raising of vitamin- and mineral-rich vegetables, both for the nutritional and economic advantage to Canada.')

Following World War Two the horticultural argument in North America was not over the healthy benefits or otherwise of the vegetable, but over where the kitchen gardeners stood: were they in favour of organic gardening or a chemical gardening? During the dust bowl disaster of 1935, millions of tons of topsoil were blown off the heavily fertilised fields of the American west, ruining many farmers. It triggered the beginnings of a crisis of confidence between the consumer and the chemical fertiliser industry. The campaigning New Yorker Jerome I

Rodale (1898–1971: the *New York Times* hailed him as the 'Guru of the Organic Food Cult') and his experimental organic farm in Pennsylvania; Rachel Carson's seminal book, *Silent Spring*, and growing concerns over sources of environmental pollution from nuclear fallout to farm pesticides moved the argument along in favour of the organic gardener. It was not long before a new kind of store, designed to cater specifically for those who were concerned about their health and the origins of their food, began to pop up: the wholefood and health food shop.

By then the UK had established, in the aftermath of World War Two, a health service free to all. It would see western medicine place its faith firmly in pharmaceuticals and surgery, and the neighbourhood herbalist, who had traded on every high street in the country before the war, packed up their plants and potions and went away taking with them twenty centuries of wisdom. Fifty years later researchers for the World Health Organisation found that 80% of people in the developing countries still relied on traditional (that is medicines largely involving plant extracts) medicines. This reservoir of knowledge surrounding vegetable and plant-based remedies was not to be ignored and when, in 2013, the late health guru Dr Michael Mosley advocated a low carbohydrate diet, rich in Mediterranean vegetables, olive oil and nuts, he was only repeating the views of ancient Indian, Egyptian, Chinese and Roman physicians from centuries before.

POPEYE THE SPINACH MAN

One vegetable whose healthy benefits were unknown to the Greek and Roman medics was spinach. It arrived from Persia in the sixth century, but the American Elzie Segar had no doubts about its positive properties when he began sketching out a cartoon character to woo Castor Oyl. This was the muscle-bound hero, Popeye the Sailor Man, who was 'strong to the finich, 'cos I eat me spinach'.

Spinach (we now know) is rich in lutein and zeaxanthin which, like the more familiar betacarotene, are antioxidants that help to combat free radicals, the molecules that are especially damaging to the proteins in the lens of the human eye and contribute to eye cataracts. Popeye, with his fine eyesight was appropriately, if inadvertently, named.

TOP FIVE

VEGETABLE APHRODISIACS

1. Artichokes
2. Potatoes – but only early varieties.
3. Lettuce – useful as a cure for impotence.
4. The *pomme d'amour* or tomato.
5. The turnip: 'it augmenteth the seed of man and provoketh carnal lust,' insisted Sir Thomas Elliot in 1539

THE VEGETARIAN MOVEMENT

'We must cultivate our garden,' declared the witty French writer M. de Voltaire in his satirical *Candide*, published in 1759. He had a special interest in the contents of the vegetable patch since he and others including the poets Alexander Pope and Percy Byshe Shelley and the pastor John Wesley, promoted the virtues of a meat-free diet. No-one took them very seriously until 1847 when a group of Christians and physicians met up at a hospital in Ramsgate, Kent to form the Vegetarian Society. The group included the Horsells who ran the hospital on vegetarian lines, the Member of Parliament (MP) for Salford Joseph Brotherton and his wife Martha. They ditched the old term, Pythagorean (Pythagorus suggested that humanity belittled itself by killing and eating its fellow companions in the animal kingdom) and instead adopted the name from the same Latin root as the vegetable: *vegere*, to enliven and to animate.

Later that year the Manchester branch of the Society was launched with a celebratory meal of onion and sage fritters, savoury pie and plum pudding. The recipes were based on the first non-flesh cookery book, which had been published in 1821 by Martha Brotherton after her encounter with the oddly named Reverend William Cowherd. The Salford clergyman abhorred the eating of flesh. He took to the streets with his soup kitchen, distributing free vegetable soup to the poor and earnestly preached a 'live and let live' philosophy to his congregation at the Bible Christian Church. During a time when meat was expensive and food scares common, he gained a significant following. Converts went to America where Amos Bronson Alcott, father of Louisa May Alcott the author of *Little Women*, and neighbour of Henry Thoreau, and a biscuit manufacturer Sylvester Graham (who espoused a diet of raw food only) founded the American Vegetarian Society at New York in 1850. The movement attracted many nineteenth century celebrities including Annie Besant (who founded the influential Theosophical Society), the shorthand inventor Isaac Pitman, the Russian novelist Leo Tolstoy, Mahatma Gandhi and novelist and playwright George Bernard Shaw. The Vegetarians, however, were not so much pro-vegetable eaters as anti-meat. 'Animals are my friends and I don't eat my friends,' explained Shaw.

To Market

Avalanches of green artichokes and asparagus cascade across the marble counters of the *Modernismo* market hall in Valencia every spring; in Amsterdam's Boerenmarkt, red, green and yellow tomatoes, peppers and aubergines are arranged in Rastafarian-coloured patterns; fat, ripe pumpkins surround farm pickups at a Kingston, Canada country market in the Fall. Fresh vegetables always make a pretty picture, although nothing quite matches the French village market. This is a nation that knows its onions.

From the summer run of elderly Citroën vans laden with tomatoes, early potatoes and *haricot vert* in le Midi to the autumn
harvest of the Basque pimento, sold to be hung out to dry on the
half-timbered house fronts, the French are past masters at bringing their vegetables fresh to market.

The freshest vegetables are those that make the shortest journey between kitchen garden and kitchen table – the
home-grown variety. Farmer's daughter Rosemarie Watkins
remembered taking her father's stock to Hereford market in the
1930s: 'The farmers used to bring the vegetables into market.
Sometimes I'd sneak off to the shops because you usually
wanted come cheese or meat, but never vegetables: we grew all
our own.' As her friend Gladys explained: 'You didn't have vegetables that weren't in season. You had sprouts when they were
in season, parsnips when they were in season, and peas and beans
were the same. You never went out to buy them.'

Seventy years later most households shopped for, rather
than grew, their fresh vegetables and it was no longer a farm
to market affair: in the growing field of Lincolnshire leeks,
deflagged (with their tops cut) to fit their plastic containers,
were trucked across country to some supermarket distribution
centre and then driven back to those county supermarkets for
sale. Bunches of beans, ruler-straight and measuring no more
than 4 inches so they fit perfectly their cling-filmed trays, were
being flown into Europe from Ghana, Egypt and South Africa.
One UK supermarket chain was reported to be selling attractive trays of miniature vegetables tied with a blade of chives:
before they reached the chilled supermarket shelf, packaging
and chives were flown to Nairobi airport. Here local women tied
the green blades of chives around a selection of Kenyan-grown
vegetables before the finished packages were flown back to the
UK. Airborne food, however, formed a fraction of the total
air freight compared to what travelled on the tarmac: according to UK government figures, in 2016 lorries shifted more food
(326 million tonnes) than any other product, producing nearly

20 million tonnes of greenhouse gas emissions (2015 figures) as they did so.

As the quantity of packaging required to shift the food grew, environmentalists began to protest that the price of the global vegetable market was over reliant on non-renewable resources and a price too high to pay. In the late 1900s as the US began to market the genetically modified tomatoes (their inactive ripening gene left them looking fit and well long after the harvest) chefs and restaurateurs complained that produce was being selected more for shape and size, rather than taste. Supermarkets countered that the seasonless vegetable was a product of consumer choice. The rise of the supermarket to supremacy in the marketplace seemed to support their claims: in the 1970s, wholesalers had marketed 90% of vegetables and fruit in the UK. Thirty years later the supermarkets had taken over 80% of the market share. And their share was growing. Supermarkets proved to be the most successful hucksters in edging out their rivals, although there was nothing novel about competitive practices in the vegetable market.

Neither were long journey times. Emperor Tiberius is said to have had his parsnips imported to Rome from the banks of the Rhine in Germany. And the fourteenth-century market near London's St Paul's, where the 'gardeners of earls, barons, bishops and citizens sold their produce', was provisioned by foot, sail power and the plodding packhorse. The ridgeways, rivers and drove roads of England carried a steady traffic of cabbage-, garlic- and leek-mongers heading for London. The market was eventually removed because of the 'scurrility, clamour and nuisance of the gardeners and their servants.' One such nuisance were the green pea sellers. In the hungry gap between winter's end and the early harvests, the poor were entitled by law to pick green peas in the field for the pot. Some of it found its way to market. At the other end of the social scale those 'gardeners of earls, barons, bishops' were condemned for sending surplus produce to market and undercutting poorer market gardeners.

Until Henry VIII sequestered the wealth of the monasteries and redistributed it amongst his friends, the local monastery and convent gardens were a steady source of vegetables. The Cistercian order, founded in 1098 in Burgundy, France, advocated self-sufficiency in the garden and invested time and effort in good tools and efficient growing methods. The cellarer at Westminster's convent garden, for example, had to supply the monastery with fresh vegetables and herbs, hay for the floors and the *garderobes*, and rushes, mints and meadowsweet for strewing across floors. He had to look after his hedged plots, his house cows and their pasture, and his hives of bees for the honey and wax. There was always surplus produce to be sold at market or traded for seed and cuttings.

Private gardens also played their part. Head gardeners were often encouraged to supplement their income with the sale of surplus produce. At Stow Bardolph in Norfolk a contract for the head gardener of 1712 stipulated that he 'maintain and keep and furnish ... Stow Hall ... with all necessary and sufficient kitchen garden stuffe'. It also allowed him to pocket the profits from the sale of vegetables to top up his wage of £50 a year. Loudon fostered the idea in his *The Suburban Gardener* (1838): 'The raising of garden crops and small fruits such as currants, gooseberries, raspberries, and strawberries, etc will form a source of interest ... and one which, in some case, may afford a little profit.'

Vegetables were traded from country to country too. Vegetables had been shipped from France and the Low Countries across to England as early as the 1300s. One of the popular destinations was the old Westminster 'convent' garden, now the Covent Garden and one of several markets which claimed to be London's larder.

Inland journey times between the market garden and the market were driven down as roads, carts and carriages improved. They improved even more when, in the 1820s, 3,000 miles of new canal were added to the nation's transport network. The canals also improved the fertility of neighbouring fields and gardens. 'Fields, which before were barren, are now drained, and by the assistance of manure, conveyed on the canal toll-free, are clothed with a beautiful verdure,' Thomas Pennant noted in 1782 of the land around the new Grand Junction Canal between Trent and Mersey.

The railways came hard on its heels. By the 1850s, the Scottish laird wintering in the south for the London season, could, and did, expect the produce of his walled kitchen garden to be picked, packed and put on the train to London so that it might arrive on the doorstep of his Chelsea villa in a matter of hours. The transport of vegetables – and everything else – was revolutionised. 'Crowds of people and mountains of goods, departing and arriving scores upon scores of times in every four-and-twenty hours, produced a fermentation in the place that was always in action,' wrote Charles Dickens as he watched the Camden Town railway develop in 1836. 'There were railway patterns in its drapers' shops, and railway journals in the windows of its newsmen. There were railway hotels, office-houses, lodging-houses, boarding-houses; railway plans, maps, views, wrappers, bottles, sandwich-boxes, and time-tables.' The 'dung-hills, dustheaps, and ditches and gardens, and summerhouses' of the area, meanwhile, had disappeared as families moved out of town, along the lifeline of the railway, to settle in the country and grow their vegetables there.

Not that the railways were welcomed with open arms. Some were as bitterly opposed as any twentieth century motorway. 'We are too much hurrying about in these islands; much for idle pleasure, and more from over activity in the pursuit of wealth, without regard to the good or happiness of others,' mourned the poet William Wordsworth (and vegetable grower) when plans were announced for a line from Kendal to his favourite Lake Windermere.

What was done was not to be undone (at least until one Doctor Beeching radically reduced the UK railway network in the 1960s). Manufacturers promoted their proximity to the railways: 'The facilities we have on all hands – sea, canal, and rail – for dispatching Manures of our usual high standard ... enable us to ensure the prompt delivery of all orders with which we may be favoured,' promised Webbs of Stourbridge. Markets adjusted their working hours to coincide with the train deliveries and, for a century, railway traffic reigned supreme as small agricultural armies of pickers were formed in the shires to pick the vegetables fresh and send them by the wagon and cart load to the station. Gypsies and travellers followed the ripening crops from region to region and swelled the ranks of local women and children picking for the markets. In the 1970s, one Shropshire man recalled his childhood summer holidays spent picking fruit and vegetables. 'You used to be off school for four weeks picking to buy shoes and clothes to go back to school because your parents couldn't afford them. The produce used to be put in baskets and sent at night on the mail train to Birmingham, to the market there'.

In post-war Britain conditions for the vegetable pickers were little better as one former soldier recalled. Returning to East Anglia he joined a government agricultural scheme which gave him work on a local market garden. 'In the army we'd dreamed of returning to 'Blighty' and perhaps running a little country pub somewhere. Instead, I found myself picking Brussel sprouts for the London train, in driving snow up on the cliff top above West Runton and crying with the cold. It was all hand work and in all weathers. We had a horse drawn hoe for the currant crop, but carrots and turnips were hoed out by hand, and beet was topped and tailed with a sickle.' Both the Shropshire lad and the demobbed soldier were picking fruit and vegetable for the bustling city vegetable market. But by the end of the twentieth century most fresh vegetables were being sold by the supermarkets.

They had started off quietly enough. In 1869 John Sainsbury and his wife established a shop in Drury Lane, just down the road from Covent Garden market in London. One hundred and thirty years later, his business had become the third largest supermarket chain in the UK. In the early 1900s a young barrow boy, Jack Cohen, was working in the London markets. He turned a small profit selling surplus army rations and in 1924 bought a supply of tea from one T.E. Stockwell, sold it again at a profit, and founded a small company using the initial letters of his tea supplier with his own surname to create Tesco. A visit to America convinced him that the self-service store was a thing of the future and that extending his lines to include non-food stuffs would create a kind of 'super market'.

As the new generation of Sainsburys and Cohens firmed up global networks of fresh vegetables, the trend was clear: the high street greengrocers and the neighbourhood shop were in free fall. Their numbers, 113,000 in 2003, had dropped by almost 20% in ten years: during the same decade the floor space of the major supermarkets had increased by 50%. Fruit and vegetables were a profitable trade and one worth competing for. With an average mark up of 40% on fruit and vegetables, the produce aisle of the supermarket was now the most lucrative part of the store.

But the world-wide market, created to fill the shelves as profitably as possible, had its critics. One was the Indian activist, Vandana Shiva (born 1952) who claimed that a global monoculture was being forced on people 'by defining everything that is fresh, local and handmade as a health hazard. Human hands are being defined as the worst contaminants, and work for human hands is being outlawed, to be replaced by machines and chemicals bought from global corporations.'

Supporters of her views, insisting that quality was being sacrificed for quantity, spurned the supermarkets and patronised farm shops, local markets and vegetable box schemes where householders bought only locally available vegetables which were in season. Only time will tell if the small, local vegetable producer will survive or go to the wall under pressure from the supermarket supremacy in fresh veg.

London's Larder

Covent Garden was the once largest fruit and vegetable market in the UK. Until the 1600s, grain grew in the fields and vegetables in the gardens that surrounded the convent of St Peter of Westminster. The convent had been built on an old Saxon site, part of a ninth-century settlement called Lundenwic and one which was regularly threatened by Viking invaders sailing upriver to plunder the town. The convent grounds declined after the dissolution of the monasteries by Henry VIII in 1500s, until a London developer, the Earl of Bedford, proposed a radical experiment in town planning. With the enthusiastic support of King Charles 1, the Earl persuaded the most important architect of his day, Inigo Jones, to design a classical public square. Drawing on his knowledge of the geometric Italian *piazza*, Jones demolished the winding alleys and lanes of the immediate neighbourhood and introduced the formal square to the people of London. As the convent gardens were buried beneath the foundations of the smart new town houses and Jones' classical church of Saint Paul, the public spilled into the square to admire his work. Unfortunately for the Earl of Bedford, the public nature of the square was its undoing and the wealthy, having so recently moved in, were soon moving out again to more private, neighbouring squares.

As the rich moved out, the fruit and vegetables moved in. A small market had stood here in 1649 surrounded by bordellos, coffee houses and Turkish bathing houses. It expanded gradually until, by the 1830s, it could rightfully claim to be the larder of London. At its height Covent Garden employed over a thousand porters and barrow boys. 'The wall-like regularity with which cabbage, cauliflowers, and turnips are built up to a height of some twelve feet is nothing short of marvellous,' enthused the Victorian writer Charles Dickens. In 1886 Covent Garden Market opened a new Floral Hall and market gardeners and country house head gardeners alike fed the market their produce.

In 1974 the old Garden was replaced by new one at Nine Elms in Vauxhall. Conservationists led a successful campaign against plans to redevelop the Garden and the old vegetable market was turned into the tourist market it is today.

A GOOD IDEA AT THE TIME: THE ONION SELLER

It was an inadvertent, but briefly successful marketing ploy by Breton onion growers which led to the French stereotype of a garçon in a striped vest, sailor's trousers and black beret precariously riding a bicycle with a baton of bread under his arm and a string of onions across the handlebars.

Times were hard in Brittany *l'entre-deux-guerres,* between the two World Wars, and nowhere more so than on the north coast of Brittany in the onion growing region around Trégor. Here the young men wore the Breton beret, and the sailors their striped shirt just as their fathers and grandfathers had before them. But unlike their forefathers the young men were prepared to travel away and earn some money. In late summer when the famous Breton pink onions were harvested around Roscoff young men would borrow the family bike and, carrying as many strings of onions as they could across the handlebars, ride down to the fishing ports of Saint-Brieuc or Tréguier to hitch a ride to the English ports. The traditional *journee d'Albion,* or the journey to Albion, brought early onions to the English south coast sellers in what was mistakenly assumed by the cartoonists of the day to be the traditional French costume. In 2004 Roscoff opened a museum dedicated to the 'onion johnnies (English buyers, tongue tied over the Breton Yanns and Yannicks who came to call, resorted to 'Johnny').

VEGETABLES PRESERVED

In the early 1800s the French navy, under blockade from the British, set sail from the port of Brest with a secret weapon on board. Hidden below decks were rows of glass *champenoises*, champagne bottles filled, not with fine wine from that region, but beans, peas and boiled beef in gravy. The bottles were kept sealed for three months before they were opened and their contents sampled. While the beef tea was judged rather weak, the beans and peas were considered to have all the freshness and flavour of new picked vegetables – high praise from a nation which traditionally cast a hyper-critical eye on the quality of their vegetables.

The bottles had been prepared by Nicholas Appert, a chef and confectioner who invented the process of canning vegetables, fruit and meat. Born at Chalôns-sur-Marne on the edge of the Champagne region in 1750 where his father worked as a brewer and innkeeper, Appert died in 1841, his culinary contribution all but forgotten. Not until a French postage stamp was issued in his honour in 1955 was Monsieur Appert's genius acknowledged.

Appert had moved to Paris in 1781 and begun experimenting with preserving food, filling his champagne bottles with different vegetables, fruit and meat and standing them in hot water before sealing them. After the success of the naval sea trials Appert, now living at Masy near Paris, set up the world's first canning factory – except that he was still using bottles, specially made to his design and stored in canvas bags to protect his workers from flying glass, should a bottle explode. His little factory was filled with cauldrons and copper boilers, kitchens and cold stores, bottle racks and cork stoppers, all devoted to storing and preserving food in such a way that the consumer could enjoy 'the month of May in the heart of winter' as his patron Grimod de La Reynière put it.

The business went well: forty women worked in the factory during the busy vegetable harvest and Appert's preserves sold in the Paris shops. The commercial potential of Appert's invention began to dawn on French government officials: preserved French vegetables could be sold for export; naval vessels could stay at sea longer; and food would no longer have to be preserved with sugar, which, under the British blockade, was in short supply. Appert, always generous with his research, was commissioned by the government to reveal the secrets of his process. But just as his book, *L'Art de Conserver Pendant Plusiers Années Toutes les Substances Animales et Végetales,* appeared in 1810 a Londoner, Peter Durand, patented the process and a London engineering company began preserving food by Appert's methods, using cans rather than bottles. Appert's own business floundered until in the 1830s he found the finance to set up another factory to bottle and can vegetables. By now the competition was too intense; the business failed and Appert died in obscurity and poverty. The French may have temporarily forgotten Appert, but they did not forget his bottled vegetables, still a staple line in French food shops today. Shelves of bottled and canned vegetables, however, were about to make way for a new piece of equipment in the store, the freezer cabinet.

The post war vegetable, served as a 'meat and two veg', was a poor and watery thing. A 1950s author who offered sensible advice on travelling etiquette – 'if talking with strangers leads to further conversation, it should remain impersonal' – also offered useful advice on cooking vegetables: 'Vegetables, Boiling. All vegetables grown above ground should be boiled with the lid off the saucepan whilst those grown under should have the lid kept on.' She was not going to advocate the art of steaming vegetables or celebrating the vegetable in the French fashion where each course of vegetables was served and savoured separately. New frosted vegetables were about to change all that.

What Eleanor Birdseye missed most about life as a fur trapper's wife in Labrador in the early years of the 1900s was fresh, green vegetables. She lived with her husband, Clarence or Bob as he preferred to be called, and their son Kellogg in a three-roomed cabin 250 miles away from the nearest store or doctor. Bob, born in 1886 in New York, had dropped out of Amherst College in Massachusetts because his family could not afford the fees. For a brief period he took a job with the US Department of Agriculture, but, always the risk taker, he persuaded Eleanor that there was a better living to be had from fur trapping. They moved to their lonely shack in north-eastern Canada and they lived off home-frozen food. Bob Birdseye had learned quickly what the native north Canadians already knew: that meat tasted better if it was frozen fast. Fish, rabbit, duck and other game, naturally frozen outdoors in the Arctic winds that drove the temperatures down as low as -50 degrees centigrade, kept its flavour. 'The Eskimos had used it for centuries. What I accomplished ... was merely to make packaged frozen food available to the public,' he would say later.

To please Eleanor, Bob experimented with freezing vegetables. He stored cabbage brought by boat in barrels filled with salt water. 'Fresh' cabbage was then hacked out of the ice when required. In 1917 the family returned to the United States and Bob Birdseye borrowed the corner of an ice cream factory in New Jersey where, in an effort to 'reproduce the Labrador winters' by means of ice blocks, brine and an electric fan, he set up business selling frozen fish. The business went bust. The Birdseyes moved on, this time to the fishing port of Gloucester where the tenacious entrepreneur experimented with quick freezing meat, fish and vegetables. He built an automatic freezer which could fast freeze food when it was placed between metal plates that had been cooled to -40 degrees centigrade with calcium chloride brine. After patenting the process and setting up a new business, the General Seafoods Company, Bob Birdseye concentrated on improving his methods. Convinced of the need to freeze vegetables when they were still fresh, he mobilised his quick freezer, mounting it on the back of a truck and driving it out into the fields where he could freeze the vegetables as they were picked. But business was slow and, at one point, he and

Eleanor had to hock their insurance policies to keep it afloat. It was just as well since he would shortly receive what was then the largest single sum of money ever paid for a single process, $22 million.

The pay-off came by chance. Marjorie Merriweather Post, the daughter of a food processing company owner, was the richest woman in America, wealthy enough to build herself a Palm beach, Florida property, Mar-a-Lago (later bought by US president Donald Trump) in the 1920s. She had been taking a yachting holiday on the Massachusetts coast when, one evening, her chef served her roast goose bought in Gloucester from the General Seafoods Company. When she learned that the fresh goose was actually several months old, she made an appointment to see Bob Birdseye. Three years later Bob's company was bought out by her family's firm and in 1930 the name changed to BirdsEye.

The millionaire Birdseyes settled into a new home where they could indulge their passion for horticulture. Bob was interested in hydroponics and believed there was enough growing space on the roofs and in the cellars of New York to feed the whole city with fresh vegetables by this method.

For the BirdsEye company, however, business was an uphill struggle. The frozen product might have revolutionised the processing of fresh vegetables, but storekeepers had to be persuaded to make room for a frozen food cabinet and housewives to add a freezer to their list of desirable white goods. 'There wasn't fridges or freezers, although the women used a bottle a lot,' recalled Don Glead, a Herefordshire countryman raised in the 1930s: 'The women used to bottle a lot [of vegetables]. Then you had all your winter and spring greens. Carrots, parsnips, potatoes, swedes, they were clamped in the winter, beetroot too: you dug a hole, lined it with straw and in they'd go.' Many housewives were reluctant to invest in a freezer, not least because they were convinced that 'frosting' vegetables was merely a means of preserving second grade produce. But they had to concede that 'frosted peas' seemed to taste sweeter than fresh peas. (It was true: frosted peas continue to convert starch into sugar even when frozen.)

BirdsEye persisted, confident that a food revolution was on the way. Even in the 1930s they predicted that a day would come when the public would buy their food from a central store where butcher, delicatessen, greengrocer and fish shop were amalgamated. Who, asked the food writers, would welcome such a development? And why would anyone want to eat frozen peas at Christmas or 'fresh' fish, which was six months old? A glance into any supermarket trolley today tells its own story.

A GOOD IDEA AT THE TIME: THE ICE HOUSE

In the UK where, on average, every person eats over 1kg of frozen peas a year, the pea is one of the nation's favourite vegetables. Freezing farm peas is a stop-watch affair where the grower has precisely 150 minutes to get the peas picked and chilled before they start to deteriorate. But long before Bob Birdseye patented his frosted food process, kitchen gardeners were rushing fresh vegetables to the ice house. Popularised by Charles II, who had an ice house built in St James Park in 1600, the ice house was all the rage among the country set of the 1700s and 1800s.

Built of stone or brick and set in the ground or the side of a hill, the pit of the house was filled with ice cut from some neighbouring lake during the winter. Packed down and kept dry, the ice would be preserved for twelve months or more. The chamber above the ice was lined with chilled shelves and rails where fresh vegetables and foods were stored until needed. But, while the gardeners on estates like Dundas Castle, Scotland and Heveningham House, Suffolk were justly proud of their state-of-the-art nineteenth-century ice houses, ice had been used to chill food by the ancient Chinese and, remarkably, the Mesopotamian gardeners 4,000 years earlier. And Alexander the Great is said to have had trenches dug and filled with mountain snow and covered with branches at Petra so that his soldiers could still enjoy cool wine, fruit and vegetables even in the heat of summer.

A Vegetable Calendar

February
In the Saxon calendar, February was the month of the cabbage.
2.   An old country saying suggested this was the first day to sow peas, but only if the weather was wet.
9.   Birthday plant of the day is the leek. To eat leeks is to suffer humiliation.
17. Birthday plant is the pea, symbol of respect.

March
1.   St David's Day when the leek is traditionally worn by Welsh people. St David instructed his brothers to wear a leek when they went in to battle against the Saxons.
1.   An old country saying suggests this was the last day to sow peas.
Ash Wednesday – the traditional day to eat parsnips for those observing Lent.

April
Good Friday – the day to plant potatoes once they have been sprinkled with Holy Water.

May
National Asparagus Month in France.
6.   Lady day traditional day to pay the allotment rents.

June
11. National Asparagus Festival in France.
13. Birthday plant of the day was the potato, the symbol of benevolence.

21.   Time to lift your tree onion.
21.   The last day for cutting your asparagus.
21.   The arrival of the first crop of peas, 'harbinger of summer,' according to Shirley Hibberd.

JULY

25, 26, 27.   The World's biggest garlic festival at Gilroy, California.
26.   St Anne's Day and Garlic and Basil fair at Tours in France.

AUGUST

Annual Potato Festival at Alliston, the potato capital of Ontario.
3rd weekend. Onion Festival, Roscoff, Brittany.

SEPTEMBER

Tomato Festival at Château de la Bourdaisière, Montlouis-sur-Loire, France.
Potimarron (a Japanese squash) Festival at Lunéville, France.
1.   Feast Day of Saint Fiacre, patron saint of the spade.
19.   Birthday plant is the cabbage, symbol of profit and gain.
27.   Birthday plant is the dandelion, symbol of bitterness and grief.

OCTOBER

2nd Monday in the month. Thanksgiving Day in Canada and pumpkin pie is on the menu.
Halloween – scoop out a pumpkin, set a candle inside to keep out the dead.
31.   Birthday plant is the nettle, symbol of spite.

NOVEMBER

Annual display of unusual vegetables at Saint-Jean-de-Beauregard, France.
4th Thursday in the month. Time to eat pumpkin pie during the US Thanksgiving Day.

DECEMBER

21. Place an onion under your pillow and you will dream the face of your future wife.
21. The shortest day – the time to plant the tree onion.
22. According to the Roman Columella, early cucumbers could be raised by cutting the down stem of a fennel or bramble and slotting the seed of a cucumber into the pith of the mother plant shortly after the winter equinox.

5

Vegetable Passions

THE POLITICAL POTATO

'I do not hear that it hath been yet assayed whether they (potatoes) may not be propagated in great quantities, for food for swine or other cattle.' So wrote John Worlidge in his *Systema Agriculturae* in 1669. 'They are much used in Ireland and America as bread and may be propagated with advantage to poor people.'

Nowadays we all like our potatoes. People in Peru like them too: they have been eating them for 5,000 years. Four thousand-year-old shards of pottery from the region suggest they worshipped, or at least venerated, the crop as well. The potato, since it became one of the world's top nine, is eaten by more people now than ever before. Yet the fried fish shop was nearly deprived of what Winston Churchill called its good companion

– fried, chipped potatoes – by those two other bedfellows: superstition and religious intolerance. 'No potatoes. No Popery' ran an election slogan in 1765. Across the water in Ireland one variety was dubbed the Protestant 'because we boil the devil out'. How on earth did this genial little tuber cause such offence?

Britain in the 1600s was a troubled place of puritanism and superstition. Country women were still being persecuted for witchcraft: Alice Molland from Exeter in the West Country was hanged for witchcraft in 1684. During the Civil War of the 1600s, with royalty and parliament on opposing sides, families were divided, churches were burned and books destroyed. The works of the devil were all around for those who could see it. The suspicious turned their gaze on the naked little potato with its voluptuous curves and suggestive shapes, not to mention its habit of multiplying and swelling when buried like a corpse in the cold ground. Clearly this too was the work of Beelzebub. The fact that the Bible made no mention of the potato further heightened suspicion especially amongst Scottish and Irish Protestants.

The Catholic communities, however, were prepared to tolerate the vegetable provided it was ceremoniously planted on Good Friday and liberally sprinkled with Holy Water to keep the devil at bay. By the mid 1700s vegetal battle lines had been drawn between the Catholics who enjoyed their potatoes and the Protestants who preferred their parsnips: during an election campaign at Lewes in Sussex, the Protestant candidate openly condemned the Catholic opposition for its popish preferences and potatoes.

It did not help the potato's cause that eating them raw often brought on eczema, which was thought to be a form of leprosy. Not surprisingly one David Davies was predicting in 1795: 'Though the potato is an excellent root, deserving to be brought into general use, yet it seems not likely that the use of it should ever be normal in the country.' John Evelyn sensibly advocated eating the fruit pickled as a salad, but it was the

Reverend Gilbert White, one of England's early potato growers, who recorded a turning point for the vegetable. He noted on 28 March 1758: 'Planted 59 potatoes; not very large roots.' A decade later in 1768 he observes: 'Potatoes have prevailed in this little district, by means of premiums, within these twenty years; and are much esteemed here now by the poor, who would scarce have ventured to taste them in the last reign.'

The Germans, after a reluctant start, were won over by the potato following a famine in Prussia. Frederick the Great (1712–1786) sent in free potatoes (and armed soldiers to persuade the peasantry to accept them) and the citizens of Offenburg in Germany were so delighted by the arrival of the potato they erected a statue of Sir Francis Drake, holding a potato, in the town square. (Drake was incorrectly believed to have introduced the potato to Europe. The Nazis destroyed the statue during World War Two.) In France, however, the potato suffered a slow start. In the 1700s the peasantry struggled to survive a boom-and-bust economy. In the good years they survived. In poor years they starved on a diet of grass roots and ferns. Courtiers who tried to intervene on their behalf gossiped that Marie Antoinette, Louis XVI's queen consort, had shown a lack of empathy, and remarked: '*Qu'ils mangent de la brioche*' – 'Let them eat brioche' (a rich butter and egg cake). The story is apocryphal, however, an army pharmacist, Antoine-Augustin Parmentier, had a better idea – '*Qu'ils mangent des pomme de terre*'. Let them eat the earth apple or potato. As a former prisoner-of-war in Prussia Parmentier had survived on a diet of potatoes and he was determined to introduce it to his motherland on his release. He began by trading on Marie Antoinette's vanity, persuading her to adorn her hair with a delicate, white potato flower. [An alternative version has it that Louis himself wore the potato flower as a buttonhole: whoever wore the flower did the trick – the courtiers fawned in admiration.] The gourmets at court were further intrigued when Parmentier arranged a dinner at court where every course included *pomme de terre*.

In 1770 he dealt Gallic prejudice to the potato the final *coup de grace* when King Louis allowed him to plant a field at Versailles with a top-secret crop of his precious *pomme de terre*. Guards were posted ostentatiously around the field to protect the crop. The security arrangements doubled people's curiosity and, under cover of darkness, the field was raided again and again. Citizens passed the illicit potato from hand to mouth. The potato had arrived at last and, as if to emphasise the fact, French revolutionaries dug up the Tuileries gardens and planted them with potatoes in 1793, shortly after they had executed Louis XVI with Doctor Guillotine's admirable new invention. Parmentier is remembered still in French dishes such as *Hachis Parmentier*, a meal of minced beef covered with mashed potato.

Back in Britain the potato was receiving a more favourable press. In 1838 William Cobbett observed in *The English Gardener* that the potato 'does very well to qualify the effects of fat meat or to assist in the swallowing of quantities of butter. There appears to be nothing unwholesome about it, and when the sort is good, it is preferred by many people to some other vegetables of the coarser kind.' It was already offering salvation to those in the poor, Celtic west of the British Isles. In Wales the labourer paid his *dyled tato*, a debt of labour, to the landowners who permitted him to grow his *tatws* on their land.

When any vegetable becomes central to the economy of a country, it develops its own customs, terms and traditions. This was certainly so in Ireland. By the early 1900s Irish families were still sharing their meal of potatoes from the *skib*, the shallow wickerwork bowl which acquired a variety of poetical regional names including the scuttle (County Clare), the *ciseóg* (County Galway) and the sally saucer (County Louth). The spud, which seems to have acquired its nickname from the broad-pronged fork or 'spud' used to raise the crop, was eaten by Catholics and, eventually, by Protestants alike. Favourites included Epicure, Red Elephant and Champion, 'whilst Arran Banners were fed to the pigs,' reports to Olive Sharkey in *Common Knowledge*. But in the late 1700s, the escalating Irish population of 8 million souls was putting severe pressure on the subsistence smallholders and their lazybeds of potatoes, planted on the bogland margins. The lazybed was a raised bed, 1m, or three stalks, wide, bordered by a narrow trench. The seed potato was cut in half and planted in March or April with a dibber or dibble. In Cavan and the midlands, the dibber was the *stibhín* and it was the job of the woman of the house who would let it be known that she was out 'guggering' (from *gogaire,* making holes for spuds). Earthing up or *lánú* where soil from the trench was scooped up and spread across the ridge was carried out three weeks after sowing and again a month later. The crop was regularly sprayed against blight with a mixture of bluestone and washing soda. Although the cause of blight was not yet understood the garden author James Shirley Hibberd blamed the grower: 'Somebody sees it every year; it comes in autumn, it generally comes after wet weather, and *mark*, the most careless growers suffer the most from its attacks. But if some one now lamenting that he has lost half his crop, should rise up and say he bestowed every care upon it, I should say – "You didn't".'

In reality the cause was a fungal-like disease, *phytophthora infestans,* that attacked the haulms before spreading to the tubers. The failure of the Irish potato crop in the 1840s became a national catastrophe and the subsequent famine killed a million and drove another 2.5 million on to the emigration ships. Cobh near Cork, the port where the potato had first landed in Ireland was, for many Irish people, their final glimpse of home as the 'coffin ships' bore them off on the twelve-week voyage across the Atlantic.

'When famine and disaster came upon that unhappy country its citizens took shelter under the Stars and Stripes,' wrote the garden author Edward Bunyard almost a century later. 'There they fanned the dying embers of hatred against the old country with a result that is with us today. No one ... will regard a potato as a mere vegetable, but rather as an instrument of destiny.'

The potato had destroyed the heart of a nation: it was soon to transform the look of the countryside. Ireland's regime of inflated rents, unmanageable mortgages and systematic evictions was unsustainable and, eventually, land reform saw almost three-quarters of the land redistributed among former tenants. While bankrupted owners abandoned their manor houses and walled kitchen gardens, large farm holdings were reorganised so that the fields formed a convenient series of rectangles spreading out behind the farmhouse, the so-called 'ladder farms', still a familiar sight in Ireland today. The political potato had caused religious intolerance; saved nations from starvation; and even altered the lie of the land.

TOP FIVE

NATIONS GROWING POTATOES

1. China

2. India

3. Ukraine

4. Russia

5. United States

Source: Wikipedia, 2022. Following Russian aggression against Ukraine, potato exports rose briefly, but most observers predicted difficult times ahead as the conflict continued.

WAR-WINNING VEGETABLES

Towards the end of World War One some people in Britain were very, very hungry. Not everyone, however. Those with money to pay the rising food prices ate well enough; those without faced starvation. There had been food shortages in the US too. As the price of a New York onion rose by 700% housewives first took to the streets to protest, and then to their gardens to dig. Public parks, golf courses and vacant lots fell to hoe and spade in a wave of community gardening. Posters exhorted the nation to 'Sow The Seeds of Victory' and, for the first time, the message went out to the American public: eating greens does you good. America joined the war against Germany on 6 April 1917 and President Woodrow Wilson reminded his people: 'Everyone who creates or cultivates a garden helps. This is a time for America to correct her unpardonable fault of wastefulness and extravagance.'

A National War Garden Commission went into top gear declaring on its posters 'Every Garden a Munition Plant', and offering free books on gardening, canning and drying. 'Can Vegetables and Fruit – and Can The Kaiser Too' read another poster. The unrestrained enthusiasm for turning every available piece of greenery into a vegetable plot was not shared by all. The Department of Agriculture regarded the work of the War Garden Commission as amateur interference into what was properly the province of farmers, but despite their lobbying, 1,500,000 children had enrolled into the United States School Garden Army by the end of war in 1918.

On the Front Line in France, meanwhile, the leek had come to the aid of the war effort. The gardens at Versailles were sown with leeks – over 25 million in 1917. When the seedlings were large enough for transplanting they were ferried by military trucks to the Front and replanted close behind the Allied army lines to be grown on and fed to the fighting troops. War-torn Britain was busy with its own private and public vegetable gardens too. 'Under DORA', the Defence of the Realm Act, local government requisitioned land to increase the number of allotments from 600,000 to 1.5 million with their campaign Every Man A Gardener. The King, who had hastily changed the Germanic family name from Saxe-Coburg-Gotha to the more English Windsor, patriotically ordered the replacing of the decorative geraniums in the flower beds facing Buckingham Palace with potatoes and cabbages. The Church of England gave special dispensation for its congregation to work on Sundays and the number of vegetable allotments trebled. With every community

in the country mourning its dead, food rationing was judged to
be politically imprudent, but finally, in 1917, it had to come in.
By this time shoppers on the streets of Berlin in Germany were
lucky if they could buy potato peelings.

In August 1918 the lawns of London's Kew gardens yielded
nearly 30 tons of potatoes and three months later on 11
November at 11.00 a.m. the Germans surrendered. Britons had
managed to home-grow a startling 2 million tons of fresh vegetables. Many an injured soldier returned to nurse his wounds
and cultivate his allotment when hostilities ceased. The rest and
recuperative value of vegetable gardening was especially important to returning servicemen, trying to overcome the nightmares
of their recent experiences.

In the US by the mid 1920s the backyard kitchen gardening
movement had begun to decline again, partly because of food
surpluses and partly because of an Irishman whose family had
been driven from their home during the potato famine. This was
Henry Ford, the man who popularised the horseless carriage,
a machine which, within a decade, saw off the daily deposit of
over 1,000 tons of horse manure on the streets of New York.
The manure had been enough to enrich every garden in the city.

The European and American economic depression of the
1930s brought the kitchen garden movement back as British
soup kitchens sold penny portions of bread and soup, and
Americans looked at subsistence gardening to help the poor.
Don Glead's father, a soldier who had survived World War One,
took on a veteran's smallholding in Herefordshire: 'We kept a
good garden, see? It was the done thing. When people'd meet,
the first thing they'd speak about was their gardens.' Publishers
marketed Shilling Guides on frugality and cheap cookery, charitable cookery and cottage cookery and there was a rush to return
to the land, to rely on Mother Nature rather than the greedy
greengrocer. However, the terrible cycle of war and peace was
about to be repeated. In the 1930s, Sunday morning was the traditional time for menfolk to tend their allotments and vegetable

plots, but on 3 September 1939 the gardens were silent. Instead, everyone was crowded around their wireless listening with impatience to a BBC programme on recipe ideas for meals from canned foods. Shortly afterwards the British prime minister, Neville Chamberlain, came on air: Britain, he declared, had called on Hitler to withdraw his invasion troops from Poland. 'I have to tell you,' he said, his speech strained, 'that no such undertaking has been given and that consequently this country is at war with Germany.' Although minutes later air raid sirens sounded out across the capital, it was a false alarm and, for the next seven months, what the French called the *drôle de guerre*, the funny war, began. Nations, meanwhile, prepared their weapons and their kitchen gardens.

In America national food surpluses had broken all previous world records. Furthermore, nitrogen was more profitably turned into explosives than garden fertiliser and the Agriculture Department campaigned against any move to 'plow up the parks and the lawns to grow vegetables'. Nevertheless, when in 1942 the Burpee Victory Garden Seed Packet went on sale, the seed trade trebled. In 1943 as canned food was rationed, the president ordered the White House lawn to be dug up and planted with cabbages, carrots, beans and tomatoes. Around 4 million Americans joined the grow-your-own vegetable brigade. (The White House lawn was dug and devoted to vegetables again in 2009 when the then president's wife Michelle Obama planted up a kitchen garden.)

Having learned their lesson in World War One, the UK government introduced rationing early on. By January 1940 households had to register at the local shops for their meagre portions of bacon, ham, butter and sugar. Soon all basic foodstuffs were rationed and the government began a campaign to turn the people into a nation of kitchen gardeners. 'Half a million more allotments properly worked will provide potatoes and vegetables that will feed another million adults and one and a half million children for eight months of the year, so let's get going and let Dig For Victory be the matter for everyone with a garden or allotment,' the Agricultural Minister declared in the stilted language of propaganda. Eleanour Sinclair Rohde, the gardening author largely responsible for promoting the herb garden as we know it today, settled down to write *The Wartime Vegetable Garden*. The Ministry meanwhile circulated cropping plans for a 'ten-rod' allotment, running Dig For Victory exhibitions and setting up demonstration vegetable plots. Every school in the country was encouraged to create its own vegetable patch, and a new, post-war generation of vegetable gardeners was born as these wartime pupils tended their 'tators and peas'.

Vegetables acquired a premium. Home guardsmen in London made hand grenades from potatoes with slivers of razor blades embedded in them. There were recipes for War and Peace pudding (made with flour, breadcrumbs, suet, mixed fruit and a cupful of grated carrot), carrot croquettes, carrot fudge, and cake mixtures made with mashed potatoes. There was Potato Pete's recipe book and Woolton Pie, named after a British government minister and made with potatoes, parsnips and herbs. There were mock potato omelettes, mock hamburgers and mock duck, the latter made with mashed potatoes, lentils, beans, sage and onion and shaped like a duck. Vegetable scraps were collected in the street to be fed to pigs raised by neighbourhood groups to supplement their rations. The nation was nervous, hungry, yet healthy. 'Most people are better fed than they used to be. There are less fat people,' declared the writer George Orwell at the time. The nation would never be so healthy again.

As the Dig for Victory campaign was launched in October 1939, Sir John Anderson, in charge of air raid precautions, gave his name to a little corrugated iron shelter which people buried in their gardens – and promptly covered with vegetables. The government used its emergency powers to increase the number of allotments to 1.4 million and forbade allotmenteers to grow ornamental flowers on them. The green sward covering the moat around the Tower of London was dug up and turned into vegetable plots by the Tower workers.

Vegetable gardening entailed unexpected risks especially for those who lived in south-east England, within reach of enemy fighter planes. One Farnham, Surrey housewife recalled:

> I was out in the garden and I could see this plane coming in. I knew it was a different one to ours from the sound of it. And next thing, there was a line of washing out, about three doors away, and he came down and he peppered all the sheets with the machine gun ... They brought him down two miles out of Aldershot and then he was put on view. Sixpence to go and have a look at him.

It was a contravention of the Geneva Convention on the treatment of prisoners of war, but perhaps understandable in the circumstances.

In 1941 The Royal Horticultural Society published *The Vegetable Garden Displayed*. (Five years later, it would be translated into German and distributed there in an effort to help the post-war reconstruction of Europe's vegetable gardens.) Americans donated 90 tons of vegetable seed and shipped them over to British allotment holders. In 1942 patriotic gardeners was estimated to be producing a record breaking 1,300,000 tons of fresh food. Did the vegetables win the war? No, but they certainly made people feel better. When canned foods came off the ration list American war gardeners could afford to relax. Yet vegetable seed sales continued to grow along with the suburban garden movement. In the early 1950s 39% of American families grew their own vegetables and 17 million self-confessed gardeners made gardening the nation's most popular hobby. At the same time in the UK around 50% of all gardens still contained a kitchen garden. Joy Davey, born in 1932, lived in Shepherds Bush: 'One half of our garden was always vegetables. We had a corner plot and a bit of a back garden – the front was for flowers, and the back for the lawn, the old Anderson and the vegetables.'

RECIPE FOR A GOOD LIFE

Growing vegetables was always considered a useful occupation for the 'lower orders'. One nineteenth-century West Midlands charity, for example, earnestly advocated including 'spade cultivation' in school curriculums and establishing allotments for their parents so that 'the moral welfare of the working classes could be promoted'. Union workhouses expected their inmates to manage a kitchen garden: 'I used to go to the Workhouse on a Friday at a certain time and fetch sixpennies worth of mixed vegetables,' recalled Katy Deem, seven years old in 1916: 'That and six pennies worth of meat for stewing was our Sunday lunch.'

Seed companies were encouraged to offer cheap or even free seed to clergymen who could distribute it amongst the poor. This is from Sutton Seed's spring catalogue of 1863: 'Seeds for distribution to cottagers. These are supplied at a reduction of about one-fourth from the Catalogue prices, with the view of assisting Clergymen and others who desire to encourage their Cottagers in the cultivation of their gardens. For this purpose we send the most useful kinds of Seeds only. Should any of our customers who desire to distribute Seeds among Cottagers not find it convenient to purchase them, we shall be glad to hear from them, in case we have any to spare free of charge.'

John Claudius Loudon had his own ideas about the improving effects of the kitchen garden on the serving classes. In a pearls-before-swine kind of declaration he wrote: 'In a state of labour and servitude, man is generally so dull and stupid, that almost every degree of refinement, or sensation beyond that of mere animal feeding, is lost on him. The rich man is happily willing to put his hand in his pocket to help him; but that merely affords a temporary relief from evil.'

The solution was simple, thought Loudon. Proprietors' should instruct their head gardeners to teach the local cottagers best husbandry. They should 'supply them with proper seed and plants, propagate a few fruit trees' and instruct the cottagers'

wives on improved modes of cookery, for example by enlivening the soup with toasted crumbs of bread, a few leaves of chives,
and a half leaflet of green celery instead of boiling the ingredients *au naturel'*. Loudon accepted that the labouring classes might
need some persuasion: 'It is astonishing how ignorant and how
extravagant the humblest classes are in these respects.' However,
enforcing improvements with 'adequate motives of hope or fear,
of reward or removal' would, he thought, prove a useful incen-
tive and help spread happiness among the poorer households
'at no additional expense to the proprietor'. 'Wretchedness and
slovenliness' would soon give way to gardens that were ornamental, neat and above all productive.

One man who supported the cause that horticulture
improved the body, the mind and the spirit, especially if you
were a member of the proletariat, was the Victorian John
Ruskin. Ruskin's life, 1819 to 1900, spanned the Victorian age.
He was a writer, critic, painter and a gardener. Reacting against
the industrialisation of society (and its products, displayed so
spectacularly at the Great Exhibition of 1851), Ruskin would
give voice to the Arts and Crafts Movement and its exponents,
who included Edward Burne-Jones, Dante Gabriel Rossetti and
William Morris. ('As to the garden, it seems to its chief fruit
is – blackbirds ... I shall set to work this morning to get some
[gooseberries] before their next sit down meal,' he wrote to a
friend about the kitchen garden at Kelmscott Manor.)

Ruskin bought a grand house overlooking Cumbria's
Coniston Water, Brantwood, in 1871, abandoning its Victorian-
style flower beds filled with blooms 'pampered and bloated
above their natural size ... torn from the soil which they loved'
and adopted instead a more natural and organic approach mar-
velling at 'what infinite wonderfulness is in the flowers and the
trees, considered ... as the means by which the earth becomes
the companion of Man – his friend and his teacher.'

Ruskin was also deeply melancholic – his wife Effy had
recently eloped with the painter John Everett Millais for whom

she had been modelling – and deeply philanthropic. One of his lifelong projects was the St George's Company which, with its stated aim being 'the health, wealth, and long life of the British nation,' was concerned that 'the British nation is at present unhealthy, poor, and likely to perish.' Ruskin was convinced that persuading the workers to return to the land and grow their own vegetables was the solution.

The Company, later renamed the Guild of St George, was designed to benefit poor, industrial workers, helping them turn away from the dictatorial factory machines and instead find fulfilment in rustic labours. They would keep the 'hills, streams and fields that God has made for us' as 'lovely, pure, and orderly as we can' and 'gather their carefully cultivated fruit in one season'. Ruskin, who put £14,000 of his own money into the Guild, expected some social improvements among the working classes to attend these good works. It would help, he thought, if the beneficiaries might make 'scrupulous use of sugar-tongs instead of fingers.'

Always under-funded, the Guild nevertheless established rural communities of working people at Totley near Sheffield, Barmouth in Wales and Bewdley in Worcestershire where 7 acres of woodland were given to the Guild by Birmingham merchant George Baker. (Baker would succeed Ruskin as Master of The Guild).

The land at Totley outside Sheffield was to be worked by a group of socialists who came together after Ruskin lectured at Ashfield in April 1876. Totley was set up as a Commonwealth under a socialist, William Hamilton Riley. 'St George has now given thirteen acres of English ground for their own,' wrote Ruskin trusting the families to rely on good work and 'no moving machines by fire' since he had a special loathing for steam engines. But the project failed and Ruskin had to send his own gardener, David Downs, to turn the operation into a fruit farm instead.

The Barmouth project was more successful. The Guild had been given property by Mrs G.T. Talbot, one of Ruskin's loyal admirers, but the vegetable plots had one drawback. The driving westerly winds, laden with sea spray, played havoc with the buildings – after one visit Ruskin promised to devote the rental income to improving them – and soured the garden soil. One of the tenants, a French exile named Auguste Guyard, came up with a horticultural solution. Guyard was a curious figure. He had been banished from France by the Church, hostile to his plans for creating a new utopian community there. Now, dressed in his grey cloak and wearing a red fez, he would stride around the village frightening small children and dispensing useful advice including the suggestion that the vegetable gardens be protected with wind breaks 'fenced with furzed hedges'.

Guyard died in 1882 and the following was inscribed upon his tombstone:

Ci git un Semeur qui
Sema jusqu' au tombeau
Le Vrai, le Bien, le Beau

Here lies a sower who
Until his death spread the seeds of
Truth, Goodness, and Beauty

The Guild outlived Ruskin and now operates as an educational trust with an environmental focus.

ALLOTMENTS FOR ALL

In Europe and America, the business of growing vegetables in allotments, garden colonies, chalet gardens and worker gardens dates back to the expansion of the cities in the 1800s. As market and back gardens were crowded out of town by the encroaching foundries, factories and mills, gardeners were forced to find land away from the home for their vegetable and flowers. In

France the poor had to make do with a *lopin de terre*, a vegetable plot squeezed into some urban corner while the more fortunate found space for the *potager* on the *jardin ouvrier*, grouped together like British allotments on the outskirts of town. The German equivalent was the *kleingarten* where rows of vegetables and flowers grew beside the barbecue, the habitable summerhouse and the social club, a model for similar garden colonies which still stretch across Europe from Prague to Paris and Helsinki to Helsingborg.

The word allotment is derived from the Old French meaning to divide out and share, although in the UK its true roots lie in an act of land theft – the enclosures. In the post medieval days most of Britain was still farmed on an open field system. By the 1500s, during the reign of Elizabeth 1, the process of parcelling up or enclosing the countryside had begun. Contrary to claims that enclosures were all for the greater good since they produced a more efficient agricultural system, enclosures robbed from the poor and gave to the already rich.

> Inclosure, thou'rt a curse upon the land,
> And tasteless was the wretch who thy existence plann'd

So declared the 'peasant poet' John Clare, a Northamptonshire countryman who witnessed the rural poor grow poorer as the surrounding fields were privatised. Even some of those directly responsible for enclosures, like this secretary to the Agricultural Board, noted with concern that 'the poor are injured, in some, grossly injured.'

Early efforts to compensate the lower classes included the idea of 'alloting' small patches of waste land for landless labourers to cultivate. In 1806 the nation's first enclosure allotments were provided at Great Somerford, Wiltshire when 970 acres were enclosed and less than 10 acres provided for allotments. As the legal Acts permitting enclosures were rushed through Parliament between 1760 and 1818, MPs were petitioned to include allotments in the enclosure Acts. But not until 1819, when the number of destitute people threatened to destabilise their communities, were parish wardens legally empowered to rent allotments to villagers. It took another twenty-six years before every Act of Enclosure was required to provide a certain number of 'field gardens' no bigger than a quarter of an acre.

Landowners, meanwhile, had gained more land, and a work-force dependent on their largess. The rural rich were troubled by the notion of allotments. They feared that a labourer with an allotment would steal their seeds. Others were resistant to people growing the products which they grew and sold. Worse still, the labourer might slyly conserve his working energies during the day, saving them up until he could expend them selfishly on his own allotment. 'The extent of the garden of a labourer ought never to be such as to interfere with his employ-ment as a labourer,' warned John Loudon. Parliament duly insisted that allotments should be small enough to prevent the labourer neglecting 'his usual paid labour'. Still, this failed to satisfy many farmers who threatened to refuse employment to any labourer who kept a parish allotment. Rising crime finally defeated them.

Hitcham in Suffolk was a pretty place, its streets lined with half-timbered farmhouses, its church decorated with a fine fifteenth-century hammerbeam roof. But the rector who preached here in the 1840s, Reverend John Stevens Henslow (1796–1861), was concerned for Hitcham's notoriety – it had one of the highest crime rates in the country. Henslow introduced allotments to reduce local crime. When farmers threatened to blacklist any labourer who would dare rent an allotment, the wise Mr Henslow launched a produce show and invited the great and good among his Victorian parishioners to patronise the show and donate prizes. The annual fruit and vegetable show, always a social leveller, had the necessary healing effect.

The industrialist Titus Salt was another exponent of the allotment. When he built Saltaire on the banks of the river Aire outside Bradford he provided 800 homes for his mill workers, each with a parlour, kitchen, pantry, three bedrooms, an outside lavatory and an allotment 'each not exceeding 15 poles in extent.' John Lawes, who patented the process for manufacturing artificial fertiliser, not only established allotments for the workers on his Rothamsted Estate, but also provided allotment holders with a club house in which he unsuccessfully tried to persuade the gardeners to drink coffee instead of beer.

The National Agricultural Labourers Union, formed in 1872, actively campaigned for allotments for its members but, although an Allotment Act was passed by Parliament in 1887, the authorities were still slow to act. The turning point, which saw the workers' frustration boil over into the ballot box, came at a by-election for Spalding in Lincolnshire in 1887. It had been considered a safe seat for the Conservative candidate until the nomination of a Liberal candidate who supported allotmenteers, Halley Stewart. When Stewart trounced his opponent at the hustings, Parliament promised to find time to consider the vexed problem of allotments. When they prevaricated further, Lincolnshire's local council elections became a battleground between allotment supporters and allotments dissenters. The supporters won and Parliament, fearing a rush of allotment MPs arriving at Westminster, pushed through changes. By 1895, at last, the number of allotments had increased by 50% to 482,901. Many were, and still are, set alongside the railway tracks. This was because the second largest suppliers of allotment ground, after the local authorities, were the railway companies which not only provided allotments for their employees, but let them out to the general public as well.

In the 1900s the allotment movement rose and fell with the economic tides. A National Union of Allotment Holders was founded in 1918 when allotments were still officially classed as being 'for the labouring poor'. In the 1930s when the Depression saw allotments in strong demand again the organisation was amalgamated with the Allotments Organisations

Society to become the National Allotments Society. In the 1980s the Society had changed its name to the National Society of Allotments and Leisure Gardeners. The change of name reflected a change of style in the allotments: new people with new passions for vegetables were moving in. Immigrant workers from the Asian, West African and Indian communities introduced their own growing skills and vegetables to the allotments. Henry Francis and Pat Garfoot were both Nottingham men with a passion for homegrown vegetables when they took over neighbouring allotments at Hunger Hill. But while Pat started out growing the traditional English vegetables his father used to grow, Henry was planting pumpkin, beans and calulu (a type of West Indian spinach) just as his parents had in the West Indies. Pat approved: 'Nowadays we have fresh vegetables to go with our regular curry nights up here on the allotments.' Then there are community allotment holders like Sue Oliver. 'My father was a London butcher and he taught me vegetable gardening on his allotment. You can't beat fresh vegetables, but my husband and I haven't the room to grow our own at home. Now we share our allotment with two other older people as part of a project to promote healthy living.'

And there are still those allotments holders who hold views little different in outlook from a century ago. Gabriel Jackson runs a small allotment in the West Midlands. 'I grow vegetables because it's part of that hunter-gatherer thing – I want to supply my family with good, fresh vegetables. Out of season vegetables in the supermarket make me angry: it takes away the pleasure of growing your own. My father grew his vegetables, his father probably did and I hope one day my son, Sam, will too. Growing veg makes you feel good.'

VEGETABLE RADICALS

Growing vegetables as a form of protest has a long and respectable past. When clothier Gerard Winstanley was ruined by the effects of the English Civil War, he was reduced to herding cattle for a living. In 1649, outraged by the poverty he saw around him, he and his community of 'Diggers' invaded common land in 1649 and proceed to dig it up and plant vegetables. 'In Cobham on the little heath the digging still goes on and all our friends, they live in love as if they were but one,' he rhymed.

Oliver Cromwell's Lord Fairfax sent in the army to deal with this vegetable riot and destroy the diggers' parsnips, carrots and beans. Another nine colonies suffered the same fate. Winstanley appealed to Cromwell, the Lord Protector for clemency: 'If the wasteland of England were manured by her children it would become in a few years the richest, the strongest and the most flourishing country in the world,' he predicted. If the poor were well fed they would soon be 'making discoveries to benefit all'; the nation could even enjoy a free state medical service, suggested Winstanley. His pleas were ignored along with his insight into a national health service and, with the restoration of the monarchy, Winstanley slipped from view to die in obscurity.

Three centuries on and a new group of diggers were in action. These were supporters of Friends of the Earth who in the 1970s organised demonstration 'dig-ins' on empty ground to highlight the fact good land was lying idle while waiting lists for allotments were lengthening. There were still 121,000 people on the allotment waiting lists in 1980 when other demonstrations began, this time against the siting of American cruise missiles in the UK. While women set up protest peace camps at one missile site, Greenham Common, the husband of one protester, Chris Mattingly, loaded his Massey Ferguson tractor and plough on the back of a trailer and hauled it off for RAF Mildenhall, a major US air base in Suffolk. Under the nose of the guards the unloaded tractor, hitched up the plough and turned over an acre of military land. A few weeks later he returned and hand sowed a crop of wheat which, in late summer, was harvested, threshed and presented to one of the aid agencies for export to a famine-struck region in the developing world, Bangladesh.

During the 1900s the pace and scale of scientific advance could be measured against the fact that, while the first manned flight had taken place in North Carolina in 1903, regular space travel was a reality by 2003. And yet throughout that century hundreds of thousands of people continued to die of starvation because they could not grow enough vegetables. Concerned by the plight of the poor and the impact of agribusiness and genetic modification on global seed stocks, a Frenchman Dominique Guillet began saving old varieties of vegetable seed in 1994.

After a spell making products for the Bach Flower Remedy company, founded in Wales in 1930, he started growing old vegetable varieties on an estate in the Auvergne. His company, Terre de Semences, was dedicated to *'la libération de la semence et de l'humus'*, the liberation of seeds and humus, although he was forced to shut down the company (and establish a seed library instead) when the French Ministry of Agriculture demanded a bureaucratic registration fee for each of Terre de Semences' 2,000 seeds. This was despite a European Union directive on promoting the production of traditional vegetable varieties and the fact that, in the last century, the West had lost 98% of its traditional vegetables. 'Let us not speak of transgenic plants: one page would not suffice to express our anger. To find and ask the true questions we would need a whole book and we have not got the time or space,' protested Guillet. 'We have far too much to do on the land so as to produce honest seeds so that growers can regain their freedom and their choice.' Terre de Semences was followed in 1999 by Association Kokopelli, an organisation devoted to saving old varieties and distributing seed, free if possible, to the developing world. Within its first two years Kokopelli had distributed 150,000 seed packets in Asia, Africa and South America.

Garden Organic, which had already started conserving mainly European heritage seeds, used around 180 citizen seed guardians to road test 'orphan' varieties for their growing seed library while in 1984, a seed gene bank was started in Norway. By 2024 the renamed Seed Vault conserved over a million items, each preserved in a waterproof aluminium bag.

The Biggest is the Best?

Ever since the Victorian clergyman Reverend Henslow started a produce show to heal tensions in his parish, such horticultural events have blurred class boundaries and bridged the social divide. And while prestigious shows like Chelsea, Harrogate and Shrewsbury attracted the upper echelons of society, the lord and his labourer were often obliged to meet and mix in the produce tent. Shrewsbury is a case in point. Established in 1857 and revived in the 1940s by the town's parks superintendent (and later TV gardening star) Percy Thrower, Shrewsbury was the fictional setting for one of literature's more famous horticultural events. In *The Custody of the Pumpkin* (1924) author P.G. Wodehouse has a pair of aristocrats, Lord Emsworth and his rival Sir Gregory Parsloe-Parsloe battling for the show's giant pumpkin prize. The competition is won by his lordship's ill-tempered gardener Angus McAllister.

However, a regular (and real life) winner during the 1920s was Mr Ruck from Shropshire. His son, Keith, himself a former head gardener and vegetable competition judge, recalled the battles that went on behind the scene. 'Father was a regular winner in the Cottagers' Class, but there was a lot of cheating went on. Like, if you got wireworm in a carrot, you'd take some soap and an old carrot, mush him up to get the right blend of colour and then use that to cure the blemish. Course when I was judging I used to look out for things like that because I knew how it was done.

'A lot of parsnips were grown in barrels, in holes 'barred' down through the soil and filled with leafmould and sand so the parsnips didn't have to fight against anything. During the shows then, the parsnips would be rested in the old bungalow baths, or zinc baths, laid on damp sacking. The parsnips were the full length of the bath and some of the tapering ends would be hanging over the end.' A showman's garden, he remembered, was not an orderly place: 'We never had a tidy garden. You got leeks growing in pipes, kidney beans growing in wire cages so they would grow nice and straight, and we were always digging into the rows so you never had anything perfect to look at.'

The growing of prize onions had a particularly deleterious effect on the appearance and the scent of the garden: 'The show onions were started in the winter, in seed. Growing onions was a sore point with my mother because one of Dad's friends was a butcher from Abergavenny who done his own slaughtering. We used to have drums of blood and soak the ground with it 'til it go near a green or a black colour. It didn't used to smell very sweet either. The show onions would be hoed before Dad went to work and again when he come home, his chief aim being to get the air to them. Then we would water with his homemade fertiliser, sheep daggin' water. He took hundreds of prizes.'

Show prizes awarded for mammoth vegetables, however, tended to attract a particular breed of gardener often, like male voice choirs and colliery bands, focused around industrial districts and workingmen's clubs. Men like prize grower Bernard Lavery of Llanharry in Wales (who once held nineteen world records and ten British records for growing giant vegetables); Mike Fortey from Cwmbran, said to have founded the UK Giant Veg movement; and record onion, potato and aubergine grower Peter Glazebrook of Halam, Nottinghamshire whose heaviest potato weighed in at 4.98kg.

ARTISTS AND THEIR KITCHEN GARDENS

Garden historians often consider artists as a potentially inspiring group of gardeners. Being creative individuals, artists are expected to bring the same visual and conceptual gifts to their gardens as they do to their art. Those expectations were fully realised in the case of Claude Monet (1840–1926), whose Normandy garden Giverny has become one of the world's most visited. Monet regularly shared his horticultural enthusiasms with a fellow Impressionist painter Gustave Caillebotte. When Monet and Caillebotte proposed visiting a friend, the friend wrote back: 'I'm glad you are bringing Caillebotte. We'll talk about gardening since Art and Literature are nonsense. Earth is the only thing that matters.'

The earth, especially that which lay beneath his *potager*, mattered greatly to Monet. He was a *bon viveur* who, like many French patriarchs, demanded daily fresh vegetables at the table. Once the art dealers were beating a path to his door, Monet could afford to purchase another house at Giverny in the neighbouring Rue de Chêne, simply for its walled kitchen garden. It was also equipped with forcing frames, a cellar for storage and mushroom growing and a fertile soil for his turnips, tomatoes, peppers and beans. A prodigious painter who worked from dawn to dusk, Monet would take time out every day to visit his vegetable garden on the Rue de Chêne and select the produce that was to be picked first thing the following day and served at his supper table.

His Impressionist colleague Pierre-Auguste Renoir, meanwhile, was overseeing the planting of his own kitchen garden in Provençe. In 1906, an ancient olive grove on a smallholding, Les Collettes near Cagnes-sur-Mer, was due to be cut down and replaced with a market garden. Prompted by the threat to the old trees, Renoir bought Les Collettes. (According to his son, the film-maker Jean Renoir, the painter was a born conservationist who would take care not to tread on even the humble dandelion when out for a walk.) The painter created a studio within the garden and while he worked, Aline, his former model and lover and now the mother of his three children, laboured in their kitchen garden. She manured the soil with grape skin, and dung from her goat, rabbits and hens, and paid special attention to their permanent artichoke beds. And when the time came, she always made sure the first pressing from the old olives at Les Collettes was ceremoniously presented to her husband.

Monet and Renoir were self-made men. Renoir had worked as a poor apprentice in a Parisian porcelain factory from the age of 13 while Monet had laboured hard and long before his paintings began to sell for serious money. Their mutual friend Caillebotte, however, was born with the proverbial silver spoon in his mouth. His fame as a painter waned in proportion to his consuming passion for gardening and when his family estate was sold, Caillebotte bought an estate at Petit Gennevilliers on the banks of the Seine, north-west of Paris, turning his Impressionist garden into a vast horticultural experiment. Aside from nurturing rare orchids, he experimented with planting arrangements, both in the flower borders and the walled kitchen garden, putting to the test the theories of Michel Eugène Chevreul: Chevreul's critical analysis of colour and his notions about complementary colours had profoundly influenced the Impressionist painters and would later influence the work of the painter turned garden designer, Gertrude Jekyll.

Monet's and Renoir's gardens have survived, along with Caillebotte's old family estate at Yerre, now a municipal park, and a section of the walled kitchen garden recreated from Caillebotte's own paintings and planted with neat rows of vegetables interspersed with dramatic strips of marigolds.

While the French Impressionists were enjoying the fruits of their vegetable patch, an English poet and an American president were sharing a passion for growing peas. The poet was William Wordsworth – his sister Dorothy frequently noted in her diary that her brother was out staking his peas. The US president was Thomas Jefferson, a keen gardener who liked to compete with his neighbours to grow the first crop of peas fit for the plate. By staggering his planting and growing at least fifteen different varieties of English peas, Jefferson could enjoy fresh peas from mid May to mid July. But a Mr George Divers usually grew the first crop and had the privilege of throwing a celebration dinner. Jefferson finally beat Mr Divers, but, in a masterful show of modestly, he kept the news to himself and dined with his supposedly victorious neighbour as usual. 'It will be more agreeable to our friend to think he never fails,' Jefferson told his family.

Finally, some of the strangest representations of the vegetable in art are to be seen in the paintings of Giuseppe Arcimboldo. Arcimboldo was born in Milan in 1527 and at 38 became a painter at the royal courts of the Hapsburgs. The artist, judging from his representational self-portraits, was a good-looking fellow, but he pursued a peculiar obsession with vegetables when he turned to the portraiture of others, in particular those of his last patron, Rudolph II. Arcimboldo had already trialled these curious vegetable portraits under the patronage of Maximilian II in 1569. In his final commission in 1591, two years before his death, Arcimboldo painted an allegorical portrait of Rudolph where the monarch's face was composed entirely of vegetables and fruits. His patron is said to have been delighted by the images.

Further Reading

The vegetable world is filled with wonderful writings from the 1600s onwards. I am indebted to all those authors who have already followed the vegetal trail – and recommend them to any wishing to continue along it.

Baeyer, Edwina von and Crawford, Pleasance, *Garden Voices: Two Centuries of Canadian Garden Writing* (Random House of Canada, 1997)

Bareham, Lindsey, *In Praise of the Potato* (Grafton Books, 1991)

Barkas, Janet, *The Vegetable Passion* (Routledge, Kegan and Paul, 1975)

Batchelor, John, *There is No Wealth but Life* (Chatto and Windus, 2000)

Beale, Catherine, *Hampton Court: A Brief History* (Hampton Court Estate, 2000)

Berrall, Julia S., *The Garden: An Illustrated History*, (Penguin Books, 1978)

Blunt, Wilfred, *The Compleat Naturalist: A Life of Linnaeus* (Frances Lincoln, 2001)

Boff, Charles, *The Big Book of Gardening* (Odhams Press, 1952)

Brown, Jane, *The Pursuit of Paradise* (Harper Collins, 1999)

Bunyard, E.A., *The Gardeners Companion* (J.M. Dent, 1936)

Campbell, Susan, *A History of Kitchen Gardening* (Frances Lincoln, 2005)

Carroll, Maureen, *They Came, They Saw, They Conquered* (RHS Journal, The Garden, June 2003)

Crouch, David and Ward, Colin, *The Allotment* (Faber, 1988)

Davies, Jennifer, *The Wartime Kitchen and Garden* (BBC Books 1993)

Devonshire, The Duchess of, *The Garden at Chatsworth* (Frances Lincoln, 1999)

Dickens, Charles, *Dombey and Sons* (Knopf, 1994)

Drower, George, *Gardeners, Gurus and Grubs: The Stories of Garden Inventors and Innovations* (Sutton Publishing, 2001)

Dudley, Stuart, *Taking the Ache Out of Gardening* (The Garden Book Club, 1962)

Dyer, Christopher, *Everyday Life in Medieval England* (Hambledon and London, 1994)

Garmey, Jane, *The Writer in the Garden* (Algonquin Books of Chapel Hill, 1999)

Gear, Alan & Jackie, YouTube (CAWR Coventry University, 26 February 2019)

Green, Candida Lycett and Lawson, Andrew, *Brilliant Gardens* (Chatto & Windus, 1989)

Griffiths, Mark, *The Times: A Century in Photographs: Gardening* (Times Books, 2000)

Grigson, Jane, *The Vegetable Book* (Penguin Books, 1980)

Guillet, Dominique, *The Seeds of Kokopelli* (Association Kokopelli, 2002)

Hadfield, Miles, Editor, *The Gardener's Companion* (J.M. Dent, 1936)

Hamilton, Geoff, *Successful Organic Gardening,* (Dorling Kindersley, 1987)

Hanawalt, B., *The Ties That Bound* (OUP, 1986)

Hellyer, A.G.L., *The Amateur Gardener* (W.H. & L. Collingridge, 1948)

Hibberd, Shirley, *Profitable Gardening* (Groombridge & Son, 1863)

Hills, Lawrence D., *Comfrey, Past Present & Future* (Faber, 1976)

Hills, Lawrence D., *Organic Gardening* (Penguin Books, 1977)

Hills, Lawrence D., *Fighting Like the Flowers: The Life Story of Britain's Best-Known Organic Gardener* (Green Books, 1989)

Huxley, Anthony, *An Illustrated History of Gardening* (Paddington Press, 1983)

Jay, Roni, *Sacred Gardens* (Thorsons, 1998)

King, Ronald, *The Quest for Paradise* (Whittet Books, 1979)

Landsberg, Sylvia, *The Medieval Garden* (Thames and Hudson, 1996)

Lawrence, Elizabeth, *Gardening for Love* (Duke University Press, 1987)

Lawrence, W.J.C., *Catch the Tide: Adventures in Horticultural Research* (Grower Books, 1980)

Laws, Bill, *Artists' Gardens* (Ward Lock, 1999)

Loudon, J.C., *An Encyclopaedia of Gardening* (Longman, Rees, Orme, Brown and Green, 1826)

Lovelock, Yann, *The Vegetable Book: An Unnatural History* (George, Allen & Unwin, 1972)

Mackail, John William, *The Life of William Morris* (Longmans, 1912)

Maybe, Richard, *Flora Britannica* (Sinclair-Stevenson, 1996)

Morgan, Joan and Richards, Alison, *A Paradise Out of a Common Field* (Random Century Group, 1990)

Mosley, Dr Michael and Spencer, Mimi, *The Fast Diet* (Short Books, 2013)

Mountain, D. (Thomas Hill), *The Gardeners Labyrinth 1594* (Garland Publishing Inc., 1982)

Moynahan, Brian, *The British Century* (Weidenfeld & Nicolson, 1997)

Parkinson, John, *A Garden of Pleasant Flowers, 1629* (Dover Publications, 1976)

Potter, Beatrix, *The Tale of Peter Rabbit* (F. Warne & Co., 1902)

Pudney, John, *The Smallest Room* (Michael Joseph, 1954)

Rackham, Oliver, *The History of the Countryside* (J.M. Dent, 1986)

Roberts, Jonathon, *Cabbages and Kings: The Origins of Fruit and Vegetables* (Collins, 2001)

Saunders, Nicholas, *Alternative England and Wales* (Nicholas Saunders, 1975)

Seymour, John, *The Complete Book of Self Sufficiency* (Faber & Faber, 1976)

Seymour, John and Girardet, Herbert, *Blueprint for a Green Planet* (Dorling Kindersley, 1987)

Sharkey, Olive, *Common Knowledge* (McPhee Gribble Publishers, Melbourne, 1988).

Shephard, Sue, *Pickled, Potted and Canned* (Simon and Schuster, 2000)

Simons, Arthur, *The Vegetable Growers' Handbook* (Penguin Books, 1945)

Smith, Tim, *The Lost Gardens of Heligan: A Brief History and Guide* (Heligan Gardens Ltd, 1992)

Smit, Tim and McMillan Browse, Philip, *The Heligan Vegetable Bible* (Victor Gollanz, 1988)

Soper, John, *Biodynamic Gardening* (Souvenir Press, 1995)

Spencer, Colin, *The Heretic's Feast: A History of Vegetarianism* (Fourth Estate, 1993)

Steer, William, *Gardening Encyclopaedia* (Spring Books, 1943)

Sudell, Richard, *The New Illustrated Gardening Encyclopaedia* (Odhams Press)

Talbot, Rob and Whiteman, Robin, *Brother Cadfael's Herb Garden* (Little, Brown, 1996)

Taylor, Gordon and Cooper, Guy, *Gardens of Obsession* (Weidenfeld & Nicolson, 1999)

Thoreau, Henry David, *Thoreau: Walden and Other Writings* (Bantam Classic, 1962)

Thunn, Maria and Thunn, Matthias, *The Sowing and Planting Calendar: Working with the Stars* (Floris Books, 2003)

Tompkins, Peter and Bird, Christopher, *The Secret Life of Plants* (Allen Lane, 1975)

Tucker, David M., *Kitchen Gardening in America* (Iowa State University Press, 1993)

Tusser, Thomas, *500 Points of Good Husbandry* (OUP, 1984)

The Victorian Garden Catalogue (Studio Editions, 1995)

White, Gilbert, *Garden Kalendar* (Scolar Press, 1975)

Williamson, Tom and Taigel, Anthea, Editors, *Gardens in Norfolk 1550–1900* (Centre of East Anglian Studies, 1990)

Woodward, Marcus, *Gerard's Herball* (Bracken Books, 1985)

Zuckerman, Larry, *The Potato* (Pan, 2000)

Acknowledgements

I am grateful to my dad and mum, Howard and Peggy, for nurturing the gardener in me and to Geof and Pauline Martin for entrusting their vegetable patch in Brighton to me back in the 1970s. For other material I am indebted to staff at the Royal Horticultural Society library, especially Jennifer Vine and Dr Brent Elliott; to staff at Garden Organic, the National Trust, English Heritage, National Society of Allotments and Leisure Gardeners, The Museum of Garden History, Sutton Consumer Products and Darren Rowe, the Ruskin Foundation, Pilsbury Company, Neil Porteous of Clumber Park, Weald and Downland Open Air Museum, Kew Gardens and the Musée des Johnnies at Roscoff, Birds Eye Foods and Bea Slizewski and Floriade in the Netherlands; vegetable gardeners at Hunger Hill, Nottingham and allotment-holders Jude Cooper, Sue Oliver and Gabriel Jackson and walled gardener David Petts; the villagers of Bucknell and the Watkins family; Sandy Green for making free with her garden and library; Julie Lachaud for her French translations; Medwyn Williams of Anglesey; and Debbie Rees at Hampton Court. The individual recollections in the book came, with permission, from the oral history archive of Herefordshire Lore and the extract from Yeats' poem is reprinted with permission from A.P. Watt Ltd on behalf of Michael B. Yeats. I am also indebted to my agents, Fox & Howard, and to the editorial skills of Jaqueline Mitchell and Hilary Walford. Thanks too to Liz Andrews, Chris Bauer, Bobbie Blackwell, Hugh Bryant, Alison Chapman, Fiona Grant, Gillian Linscott, Eileen Klotz, Michelle Seddon-Harvey, Paul and Vicki Murray, Carole Protherough, Trevor Reed, Keith and Doreen Ruck and Glenn Storhaug. I am obliged as ever to the companionable Sarah, Kahlia and Rosie, and to Abby, to whom this book is dedicated.

Index

The destination for history
www·thehistorypress·co·uk